A Companion to Tyagaraja

A COMPANION TO TYAGARAJA

A Lyric to Liberation

SUDHA EMANY

Motilal Banarsidass Publications

MOTILAL BANARSIDASS
PUBLICATIONS
4741/23, Ansari Road, Daryaganj, New Delhi - 110002 (India)
Email: *mlbd@mlbd.com* | *sales@mlbd.com* | *exports@mlbd.com*
Website: *www.mlbd.com*

A Companion to Tyagaraja
by
Sudha Emany

First Edition Published in 2022

Published in India by Motilal Banarsidass Publications

ISBN : 978-93-91759-78-0 (HB)

Printed and bound in India

To

The nameless One

Lovingly named Rama,

Humbly

Om tat sat
brahmārpaṇam astu

Acknowledgment

As before, I'd like to place on record my deep debt of gratitude to my uncle, Dr. I. S. Madugula, of Austin, Texas, for his tireless help with every tricky subtlety and nuance of the lyrics that stymie the best of translators. The challenges presented by the unique idiom of the saint are the ultimate test to which, alone, I'd have been no equal.

Table of Contents

Transliteration, Translation, etc.

1. Note on transliteration

For the Telugu compositions transliterated, the conventional Sanskrit phonetic characters and diacritics have been used. Following standard practice, *c* stands for the *ch* sound in '*ch*air,' and *ch* represents its aspirated variety.

The retroflex *ḷ* is used to represent ళ (ళ).

Long *ē* and *ō* are marked for the sake of clarity; they are always long in Sanskrit.

The segments of the lyrics *pallavi, anupallavi,* and *caraṇam* are abbreviated to *p, a,* and *c.*

In the transliteration, when combined words are separated for purposes of clarity, a break is inserted between the consonant at the end of a word and the following vowel, *e.g. kōrikal ēlāg īḍēru*, splitting the combined form *kōrikalēlāgīḍēru.*

2. *Note on the "Translations"*

The lyrics "translated" are by no means literal translations of the originals; at best they are paraphrases in user-friendly English, preserving—to the extent possible—the original flavour, spirit, and impact.

3. The term sometimes used to refer to *caraṇam* is "verse." Others use "stanza." The frequently used terms *pallavi* and *anupallavi* appear on occasion as refrain (theme) and supporting statement. *Tāla/laya* may appear as rhythm or beat or even tempo in an approximate sense.

Needless to say, anyone reading about Tyagaraja is already familiar with the basic musical terminology. The English alternatives are provided for the benefit of the novice.

Foreword

Presuming on the fact that my original volume *Tyagaraja: Lyric to Liberation* serves the instructional function of helping teachers, students, and performers of music by providing interpretation and explanation of the lyrics of the saint-musician Tyagaraja, I have decided to translate an additional 168 compositions, bringing the total number discussed to somewhat less than one half of Tyagaraja's available *kṛtis*.

The organization of the *Companion* is simple and straightforward. The entire content of the book is divided into three sections: Morals, Moods, and Meditations. However, this is not a hard and fast classification because some songs can fall under more than of those categories. Within each section, the original compositions will first be transliterated into English indicating the name of the raga, followed by the translation and a brief gloss highlighting the significant features that account for the particular appeal of that composition.

Once again, I'd like to repeat my original caveat about these translations, namely, that they are by no means strictly faithful to the original or word-for-word renderings. They are almost recreations of the spirit of the lyrics, while being intelligible to the contemporary student, teacher, or singer. However, they undoubtedly exhibit total faithfulness to the saintly bard's devotional fervour and his avowed goal of liberation.

For obvious reasons, repeated addresses to the Lord at the beginning of the songs, the signature of the composer at the end, and lists of attributes of the deity are omitted from the paraphrases.

Within the total corpus of his lyrics— be it 700 or 24,000— Tyagaraja's only aim is to offer his prayers to Lord Sri Rama in as many different ways as possible as straightforward praise, veiled criticism, plaintive request, self-deprecation, description of the deity's physical appearance, or a narration of His exploits across the eons. The only difference between one lyric and the next one is the inclusion of detail and the unique flavor created by the words deployed with a view to point the devotee toward the goal of self-realization. And it is these subtleties that we try to explicate in the saint's body of work. The very fact that Tyagaraja composed hundreds, if not thousands, of songs on the *single* theme of adoration of Rama displaying infinite variety is mind-boggling.

This work is premised on the view that the saint-musician wrote and sang his lyrics not so much for his personal emancipation as the emancipation of the ordinary man who was stuck in the impossible cycle of samsara and needed help to get out of the entanglement of desire, envy, and despair. His bhakti was not a social phenomenon; it was an individual aspiration, based on self-improvement. At the same time, it was a surefire means of salvation for the *hoi polloi*.

His music was not mere entertainment or display of technical prowess; it was a direct means of communication with the Divine.

Although the dilemma of not including some of Tyagaraja's gems in the original book has been resolved to some extent, selecting songs for this book has not been any easier.

Spellings of the names of ragas have been standardized so as to be phonetic.

Roman alphabetization is used throughout, with no distinction made between long and short initial vowels, and *s* and *ś*.

Śrī Rāma Navamī, 2022

SECTION I

MORALS

In this section are included songs that touch on the significance of moral values for the devotee in any way, shape, or form and to any degree whatsoever. It is well known that Tyagaraja did not brook the slightest misdemeanor and that he severely chastised people for their moral lapses. More importantly, in song after song, he condemned the dissimulators in the society who pretended to be great devotees while living a life of sin.

Ēm andunē vicitramunu
Raga *Śrīmaṇi*

p. emandunē vicitramunu
ila lōna manujul āḍē

a. nī mantra mahiman erungalēka
sāmānyulai palkēru nītō

c. tāmasambu cēta tatvamu palkucu
kāma dāsulai karuṇa māli madini
bhūmi sancarinci poṭṭa nimpucunu
tāmē peddalaṭa tyāgarāja nuta

How can I describe

the strange behavior of people
who know not the power of your mantra
and approach you in a worldly way

discussing Reality foolishly,
remaining slaves to lust,
heartless, eking a living,
and pretending to be role models.

Gloss
A familiar complaint of the saint, this general theme underlies his entire output of songs. Self-purification is the first step toward true devotion, or it is a sham. He has no patience for such fake bhaktas. He effectively contrasts *tāmasa* with *tattva.*

Enduku peddala vale
Raga *Śankarābharaṇam*

p. enduku peddala vale buddhi iyyavu
endu pōdun ayya rāmayya

a. andari vale dāṭi dāṭi vadariti
anda rāni panḍāye kadarā

cl. vēda śāstra tatv ārthamulu telisi
bhēda rahita vēdāntamulu telisi
nāda vidya marmambulu telisi
nātha tyāgarāja nuta nijamuga

My Lord Rāma,
why won't you teach me
traditional good conduct?
Who else is my refuge?

Like others I strayed
never achieving the fruit,

though versed in Veda
and its true import,
and the science of sounds.

Gloss
Frequently, the composer questions the Lord why He did not check him when he strayed from the straight and narrow path. After all, he knew the Veda and high philosophy, yet he missed the rewards of his learning. This is not to say that the Lord is responsible for all his misdeeds, but a recognition that he needs His grace in all that he does on a daily basis. This recognition keeps him on his toes and bonds him with the deity. He believes in the lessons taught by the ancients.

Evaraina lērā
Raga *Siddhasēna*

p. evaraina lērā peddalu
ila lōna dīnula brōva

a. bhava sāgaramuna carincu
balu gāsi rāmunitō telupa

c. kali mānav ādhamula kāryamulu
kāma matsar ādula kṛtyamulu
cala cittamu lēni vār ipuḍu
cāla tyāgarāja nutunito telupa

Aren't there any upright souls left on earth
who can rescue people from their evil ways,

and report to Rama the anguish
suffered by people enmeshed in samsara,

and the misdeeds of base humanity,

their lust and envy—
people with unfaltering minds?

Gloss

It is a basic tenet of Tyagaraja that, without a rock solid moral foundation, one can never be a true devotee, let alone achieve liberation. Hence his lament in this song that virtuous people are not doing their part in correcting the evil ways of their peers. A major rhyme in the song is *kali-ila-balu-cala.* One effect of a rhymed structure is that it is tightly bound together, without the individual ideas hanging loose.

Kaḍatēra rādā
Raga *Tōḍi*

p. kaḍa tēra rādā manasa

a. eḍa lēka bhajana jēsi nī
yeḍa kalgu nija dabbarala telisi

c. khala citta laukikam anē
śṛṅkhalam andu dagalakanē
ulūkhala baddhuniki nija dāsuḍai
velasillu tyāgarāju māṭa vini

Cleanse yourself, O Mind
through constant worship
and learn your own faults
without getting caught
in the evil ways of the world.
Listening to Tyagaraja,
devote yourself to Lord Krishna
who was tied to the mortar.

Gloss
Tyagaraja recognizes the important role the mind plays in both destroying and redeeming the inner peace of the devotee, and hence determines the success of his efforts to attain his goal. If unchecked, the machinations of the mind will rob the devotee of his peace. If controlled, the same mind will lead him to his dear Lord. All it has to do is analyze itself and keep itself pure through incessant worship.

Tyagaraja's idea here is that Lord Krishna who freed Himself from the massive mortar will unshackle us from the bonds of Samsara, so all we have to do is seek refuge in Krishna.

Kanugonu saukhyamu
Raga *Nāyaki*

p. kanugonu saukhyamu
kamalajuk aina kalgunā

a. danuja vairi yagu rāmuni
daya kalgina yatani vinā

c1. tanuv okacō
tagina vēṣam okaco
janula nēcu vāriki
jayam aunē tyāgarāja

Even Brahma does not enjoy
the happiness that I have,
sans the grace of Rama.

Will those ever thrive
that lead double lives
and parade themselves
as paragons of perfection?

Gloss

Sincerity and conviction are emphasized here, and fake devotion and dissimulation are condemned. On any number of occasions, Tyagaraja lambasts pretense as a moral shortcoming. The word *vēsamu* (show, disguise) appears frequently in the lyrics.

Kṛpālavāla kaḷā dhara
Raga *Nādavarāṅgini*

p. kṛpālavāla kaḷādhara śekhara
kṛt ābhivandana śrī rāma

a. nṛp ōttama śaraṇāgata jan āgha
nivāraṇābja hit ānvaya śaśānka

c. apavarga phala kāmamulanu jūci aḍḍamai
aṇim ādi siddhula mōsabuccedar ayya
supavitra rūpa sadā karuṇa jūḍu
sura pālaka tyāgarāja nuta

Embodiment of Grace,
revered by Siva, and of Solar lineage,

People are tempted
by miracles of great allure,
Deliver me from such delusion.

Gloss
The scriptures warn us about falling prey to cheap tricks or even so-called miracles which have nothing to do with *mukti* and are only a hindrance thereto. The seeker should be strong enough to resist their temptation, if he wants to reach his goal of Self-Realization. Tyagaraja repeats this theme often and cautions devotees against such pitfalls. Miracles do not a mahatma make.

The song abounds in beautiful compounds and sound effects. The purpose of songs such as this is to make the instruction appealing to our minds.

Kṛpa jūcuṭaku
Raga *Chāyā Taraṅgiṇi*

p. kṛpa jūcuṭaku vēḷarā rāma

a. aparādhamulan ōrva vaśamā-
yana pōkavē sari vāralalō

c. paramārthamau mārgam erugaru
prabhuvul ella nīca sēvakulurā
para lōka bhayam enta kānaru
vara tyāgarāja hṛtsadana

Now's the time, Rama,
to show me compassion,

without telling my peers that
my misdeeds are unforgivable.

The rulers know not the path,
they are but lowly vassals
who do not fear the nether world,
you who dwell in my heart.

Gloss

Tyagaraja asks Rama not to tell his peers that his sins are beyond redemption, because those people, including the leaders of the society, have no concept of Truth and Reality. As opposed to those folks, he holds Rama in his heart and has thus purified himself and deserves His mercy.

Līla gānu jūcu
Raga *Divyamaṇi*

p. līla gānu jūcu guṇa śīlula nā
pāla kalga jēsi pālimpum ayya

a. pālumālina pāmarulan olla
paramātma yī lōkamulanu

c. nara kinnara kimpuruṣ āsura
nirjara rāja śiv ādi ramā patula
taru bhūdhar ānēk ānḍamula śrī
tyāgarāja nuta śrī rāma nī

O Rama,
please let me be surrounded
by good people
who see this world as your play—
the gods, demigods, moving
and stationary entities.

I don't want to consort
with useless nincompoops.

Gloss
This again is a recurring theme in Tyagaraja's lyrics. He sincerely believes that the right company matters in his quest for the Godhead. A popular verse in Sankara's *Bhaja Govindam,* a.k.a. *Mohamudgara* reads: *trijagati sajjana saṅgatir ekā, bhavati bhavārṇava taraṇe naukā,* In all three worlds, only association with pious people can ferry us across the ocean of samsara.

Pāmarulu (idiots) and *mānav ādhamulu* (wretched, lowly humans) are frequently used by Tyagaraja to express his contempt for degenerate folks.

This song is reminiscent of Ramadas' "*sāmānyula centa ceramu,* (We will not associate with the common people.)" This is a favourite theme of his as well.

Manasā śrī rāmuni
Raga *Māra Ranjani*

p. manasā śrī rāmuni daya lēka
māyamaina vidhamēmē

a.ghana duritamulak oḍigaṭṭi nā
kāryamulu ceracitivō

c. para dārala para dhanamulak āsa-
paḍi ceḍi tirigitivō lēka
para jīvātmula himsincitivō
vara tyāgarāja nutuni maracitivō

O Mind,
what have you done
to lose the Lord's compassion?

Have you committed heinous crimes
and ruined my good works?

Or chased other people's women and wealth?
Maybe you hurt other creatures
or neglected the Lord.

Gloss
Our mind, when it gets out of control, is capable of all kinds of dastardly acts. It is our job to seize control of it back again, if we want to advance spiritually. It is this moral imperative that Tyagaraja emphasizes throughout his lyrical output. There's mild rhyming in the last verse, with prominence given to the sound *r*. All our philosophers and saints prohibit the pursuit of flesh and pelf as the two greatest distractors that hinder spiritual progress by generating negative energy and wasting valuable time in the long term.

Mariyāda kādurā
Raga *Śankarābharaṇam*

p. mariyāda kādurā

a. karuṇ ākara vārini vīrini
sari jēsi cūcuc unḍunadi

c. rāgamu tāḷamu rakti bhakti jñāna
yōgamu mari yanurāgamu lēni
bhāgavatul udara śayanulē kāni
tyāgarāj ārcita tāraka carita

It's not right
to treat all and sundry alike.

Those who do not possess
knowledge of music, piety,
divinity, and love of the Lord
only keep reincarnating.

Gloss

In this composition, Tyagaraja tells the Lord to distinguish between fake and real devotees. Real devotees equipped with the knowledge of music and a yearning for the divine can attain liberation, but not the rest. He definitely stresses the importance of *jñāna,* which can be obtained through bhakti, through the medium of the song. In the song above, Rama is praised as being impartial, but he *is* asked to differentiate real devotees from show-offs. Also, this song once again stresses the importance of devotion, aided by the music, in the cultivation of spiritual knowledge.

Mēnu jūci mōsa pōkavē
Raga *Sarasāngi*

p. mēnu jūci mōsa pōkavē manasā
lōni jāḍal īlāgu kādā

a. hīnam aina mala mūtra raktamulak-
irav ancu māyā mayam aina cāna

c. kanul anēṭi ampa kōla cēta gucci
canul aneṭi girula śiramu nunci
panulu cētur aṭa tyāgarāja nutuni
bāga nīvu bhajana cēsukommi strīla

Don’t be fooled by the female body
which within is only
blood and waste matter;

women pierce your heart
with shafts of amorous glances,
and offer their bosoms

for you to rest your head.

Worship Rama instead.

Gloss

Not sure how attractive an alternative Tyagaraja is offering to the devotee, but he is by no means alone across cultures and continents in bad-mouthing women for all of the world's problems. Religion also throws in wealth for good measure to shun if the devotee wants a smooth passage to heaven.

The saints and philosophers certainly are not misogynists. They are merely advising us that, ultimately, all the attractions of the world are evanescent and will hinder spiritual advancement. The main focus of our wisdom of the ages, in order to know the "meaning of life" and its purpose is to learn to discriminate between the temporary and the permanent and strive for the latter, which is real happiness. Temporary, circumstance-driven pleasure invariably leads to misery. And they are not talking about the controlled, purposeful social institution of marriage which is essential for the stability of the society. It is the senseless, casual attractions of the world that we have to be wary of.

Mōkṣamu kaladā bhuvilō
Raga *Sāramati*

p. mōkṣamu kaladā bhuvilō
jīvan muktulu kāni vāralaku

a. sākṣātkāra nī bhakti
sangīta jñāna vihīnulaku

c. prāṇ ānala samyōgamu valla
praṇava nādamu sapta svaramulai paraga
vīṇā vādana lōluḍai śiva manō-
vidham erugaru tyāgarāja vinuta

O Omnipresent One,

There's no final liberation
for those who are not free first
from the shackles of this world,
and for those lacking in devotion,
and understanding of music
that it is the primal energy
that's morphed into the seven notes,
even as Siva lovingly strums his veena.

Gloss

Tyagaraja invariably fuses devotion, music (including the lyrics), and *jñāna* into a unified essence that underlies the highest goal of liberation. *kīrtana* is part and parcel of bhakti. Although music and devotion are individually capable of advancing our spiritual efforts, needless to say, a combination of them is doubly effective in achieving the final goal.

Nē mora peṭṭitē
Raga *Rūpavati*

p. nē mora peṭṭitē madi lōna
nīk āyāsam ēlarā

a. ī mānav ādhamulanu kōri
ella vārala valen unḍakanu

c. tapam okaṭi yonara jēsitinō
dānamb okaṭi aḍigitinō
kapaṭ ātmuḍai palikitinō
kali hara tyāgarāja nuta

Do I upset you
if I fret within myself,
without begging lowly people,
like the others?

Have I performed penances,
asked for charity,
or engaged in vile gossip?

Gloss

There are many ways devotees can pester their deity for favours. Tyagaraja is inwardly lamenting his fate and asks the Lord here whether that constitutes harassment. It's a clever way of saying that he has been a good boy and deserves extra candy. Also, he bad-mouths wicked people and their followers at every turn, because moral uprightness is the *sine qua non* of genuine devotion. The compound word *mānav ādhamulu (mānava + adhamulu)* occurs on cue again.

Nī bhakti bhāgya
Raga *Jaya Manōhari*

p. nī bhakti bhāgya sudhā
nidhin īdēdē janmamu

a. bhū bhāramu kāni sura
bhūsurulai janincina

c. vēdōktambau karmamu
veta kalgu gat āgatamau
nād ātmaka tyāgarāja
nāth āpramēya sadā

Soaking in the elixir
of your devotion
is the only way to live
for good men or gods.

Vedic rituals generate
karma that leads to rebirth.

Gloss

By way of reinforcing bhakti toward Rama, Tyagaraja actually teaches the highest philosophy that goes to the root of the Scripture—*jñāna,* that goes well beyond karma. Karma helps purify the mind, devotion focuses it, and *jñāna* liberates it from the shackles of the "human condition." Sankara declares in *Vivekacūḍāmaṇi* (11): "Right action helps to purify the heart, but it does not give us direct perception of the Reality." (tr. Prabhavananda and Isherwood).

Nijamugā nī mahima
Raga *Śahāna*

p. nijamugā nī mahima telpa lēru

a. bhajana sēyum ani palkiri kāni
aja gaja simha sṛgāl āntaram ani

c. buddhi yanu tallini viṣaya viṭulaku
proddun osagi paikamul ārjincē
siddhulu sujanula sabhaku rā nērani
peddalu śrī tyāgarāja vinuta rāma

Those who recommend your worship
do not really fathom your power, Rama.
their understanding differs from the truth,
like the lamb from the elephant, or
the wily fox from the mighty lion.

The bogus holy men debase their intellect
And make money off it, but they
are not welcome among pious people.

Gloss

It is standard practice in Indian literatures to denigrate sanctimonious hypocrites who never practice what they preach, making them fraudsters. Also, while there were great poets who enjoyed the patronage of rulers, several others shunned that approach, on the grounds that it was sinful to "sell" their works to unscrupulous patrons for financial gain. They equated it to pimping. A famous example is Potana (1450-1510), a Telugu poet who translated the *Bhagavata,* who never dedicated his work to a royal patron, choosing to live a life of penury. Here Tyagaraja, too, expresses his contempt for the fork-tongued, janus-faced "elders" of the society, when it comes to the worship of the Lord. The use of the word *siddhulu,* literally realized beings, is highly sarcastic, giving the lyric its unique flavor.

Paralōka bhayamu lēka
Raga *Mandāri*

p. para lōka bhayamu lēka
bhava pāśa baddhul aiyēru

a. kari vāji śṛngāra rāma
śibik ādul ella manakē kaligen ani

c. konna kāntalanu kanna biḍḍalanu
vanne cīralanu vāna guḍiselanu
tinnagā kani daiva lōkam ani
tannukōḷḷalo tyāgarāja nuta

Not worried about their afterlife,
people are trapped in samsara,

deluding themselves that they
possess elephants, horses,
and palanquins;

and that their paramours,
offspring, fancy clothes, and shelters
are their heavenly habitat!

Gloss

The ignorance of people caused Tyagaraja untold grief. How could anyone not see what's in front of their noses? It's this desire on his part to uplift the common man that runs through all his lyrics in different modes that attracts our attention. When he pinpoints the delusions of mankind, he is not being a misanthrope; he is a well-wisher of humanity.

The last couplet, reinforced by the *-nn-* sound is really a cutting criticism of those deluded into thinking they are in heaven in the company of mistresses, have fancy clothes, and raise bawling babies.

Proddu poyyenu
Raga *Tōḍi*

p. proddu poyyenu śrī rāmuni pūni bhajimpavē manasā

a. niddura cēta konnāḷḷu viṣaya buddhula cēta konnāḷḷu ō manasā

c1. prodduna lēci tritāpamulanu narula pogiḍi pogiḍi konnāḷḷu
paṭṭi yeddu rīti kanna tāvula bhujiyinci ēmi teliyaka konnāḷḷu
mudduga tōcu bhavasāgaramuna munigi tēlucu konnāḷḷu
paddu mālina pāmara janulatō verri palukulāḍucu konnāḷḷu ō manasā

c2. mudamuna dhana tanayāgāramulu jūci madamu cēta konnāḷḷu
andu cedarinayanta śōkārṇava gatuḍai jāli jenduṭayu konnāḷḷu
yedaṭi pacca jūci tāḷalēka tānilanu tiruguṭa konnāḷḷu
mudi madi tappina vṛddhatanamucē mundu venuka teliyakaye konnāḷḷu

c3. yāgādi karmamu sēyavalenanu yalasaṭa cēta konnāḷḷu andu
rāga lōbhamulatōnaparādhamula jēsi rājasamuna konnāḷḷu

bāguga nāma kīrtanamulu sēyuṭe bhāgyamanaka konnāḷḷu
tyāgarāja nutuḍaina śrī rāmuni tatvamu teliyakayē konnāḷḷu

Time's passing, Mind,
let's worship Sri Rama.

People squander time in sleep
and tempting worldly pursuits,
entangled in family and possessions,
feeding off parents and consorting with the lowly,

rejoicing in the property while it lasts,
then grieving over it when it is gone,
envying the neighbours' wealth,
and will in dotage lose their wits
and won't know whether they are coming or going.

They squander time in unwise rituals
and practices, their unhealthy addiction
blinding them to the bliss
that's the Lord's name.

They don't realize that the worship of the Lord
leads them to His state that is liberation.

Gloss

Tyagaraja is never tired of pointing to his fellow-humans that they are foolishly wasting their time in senseless avocations without realizing that their time is running short. Everyone seems to waste their collective time, without once stopping to think how time's slipping through their fingers. This pains the saint who then provides sage counsel.

Rāmā nīyeḍa
Raga *Kharaharapriya*

p. rāmā nīyeḍa prēma rahitulaku
nāma ruci telusunā ō sītā

a. kāmini vēṣa dhāriki sādhvī naḍata-
lēmaina telusunā ā rīti sīta

c1. tana saukhyamu tānerugaka norulaku
tagu bōdhana sukhamā
ghanamagu puli gōrūpamaitē
tyāgarāja nuta śiśuvuku pālu kalguna

Those who have no love for you
cannot comprehend
the allure of your name.

A stage actor has no clue
to the real person he's playing,
the ignorant one unaware of his own good
cannot preach to others,
the tiger strutting as a cow
cannot relieve the baby's thirst.

Gloss
Fake devotees will never understand the true significance of Rama's name, just as an actor playing the role of a chaste woman has no idea what chastity is like; one who has never

reached his goals is not qualified to teach others what they are; and the tiger in cow's hide can never feed a baby with its milk. Another admonition is that one should practice what one preaches. If Tyagaraja talked about liberation, he had all the qualifications to do so even *before* he attained sainthood.

Samayamu ēmarake manasā
Raga *Kalgaḍa*

p. samayamu ēmarakē manasā

a. sumatulau narulanu jēri nija
sukham anubhavincuṭaku nīk idi

c. antarangamuna kalugu bhayamuna
āntarika bhakti mārgamu telisi
dānta samrakṣakuḍ aina śrī
tyāgarāja sannutuni jūḍa

O Mind,
don't miss this chance

to mix with good people
and enjoy bliss,

to overcome fear,
to see the saviour of sages,
and follow the path of bhakti.

Gloss

Associating with good people, according to teachers of philosophy, including Sankaracarya, is a sure means of qualifying for the Lord's grace. In fact, across sections of spiritual seekers, that is the starting point for a novice devotee. They learn from followers of well-known devotees, until their own status has been certified. Tyagaraja advises people not only to stay away from evil influences, but also positively seek the company of pious people. *Now* is the time to cultivate positive attitudes and practices. If nothing else, you will be at peace with yourself as well as the world. In that serene place in your heart, Rama will appear apace.

Śāntamu lēka
Raga *Sāma*

p. śāntamu lēka saukhyamu lēdu sārasadaḷanayana

a. dāntunikaina vēdāntunikaina

c1. dāra sutulu dhana dhānyamuluṇḍina
sāreku japa tapa sampada kalgina

c2. āgamaśāstramulanniyu cadivina
bhāgavatulanucu bāguga pēraina

c3. yāgādi karmamulanniyu jēsina
bāguga sakala hṛdbhāvamu telisina

c4. rājādhi rāja śrī rāghava tyāgarāja
vinuta sādhu rakṣaka tanakupa

The serene mind is a happy mind
for the philosopher and the self-controlled,
for the well-heeled householder
who worships the Lord,

and for the well-read,
the devotee, and the savant.

Gloss
This short but very popular song stresses the need for the cultivation of a tranquil mind, no matter one's occupation. The reason is simple: the first thing a devotee needs to do is to declutter his mind in order for God to set foot in it. The *Bhagavadgīta* (6.27) declares that the yogi who is calm of mind is blessed with supreme happiness.

Sarasīruh ānana rāma
Raga *Mukhāri*

p. sarasīruh ānana rāma
samayamu brōva cid ghana

a. para bhāmalan āśinci yannam iḍi
pagalu rēyi sarasam āḍu vārin olla

c. brāhmaṇīkamu bāya nīcula
bratuk āyen adi gāka yī kalilō
brahmam aina māṭalu nērcukoni
baragēr ayya tyāgarāja nuta

It's high time, Rama,
that you saved me.

I will not give up my morals
and join those who covet
other women with whom they consort,

and only talk Brahma these days.

Gloss
A recurring theme of the saint. He must have seen a lot of depravity occurring around him that pained him immensely and made him pray to the Lord to save him from all forms of wickedness and fraud. There was of course no salvation without self-purification. We have a lesson here, too, namely that evil obtains all the time, but it's our job to stay away from it with the help of moral living and sincere devotion. Tyagaraja's music is not just for listening.

Sari jēsi vēḍuka
Raga *Tīvra Vāhini*

p. sari jēsi vēḍuka jūcuṭa
sākēta rāma nyāyamā

a. dhara lōna nī nija dāsulanu
kandarpak ādula nija dāsulanu

c. kokka śastra vidulu nara sannuticē
goppa bahumatulan andēr ayya
cakkagānu bhakti śāstra vidula
cāla kani navvedaru tyāgarāja nuta

It's unfair to compare, Rama,
your devotees with those
who are slaves to passion.

Pundits in the science of love
enrich themselves by gifts,

and scoff at those
who follow Rama.

Gloss

Apparently, Tyagaraja is miffed that the Lord doesn't seem to distinguish this-worldly people from other-worldly people, even as the former ridicule the latter. Those who talk eruditely about lust seem to profit from such a pursuit, so they laugh at the devout. His only recourse however is to complain bitterly to Him and ask Him to reform the misguided.

The use of the nominal compound *kokka śāstra vidulu* (experts in the "science" of love) is a critique of the sensuous folks who are not only misguided themselves but also disparage the true devotees. Clearly, sensuality, along with other forms of immoral behavior, is the root cause of all evil in the world. It is responsible for people straying from righteousness.

Satta lēni dinamulu
Raga *Nāganandini*

p. satta lēni dinamulu vaccenā

a. satta mātramā saccitta śāyi
sākēta nilaya daiva

c. kali lōna prathama pādamulō
tali danḍri guru bhaktiyu lēka
palumāru duṣkṛtamb onarpa
valenā tyāgarāja nuta daiva

Is there no godliness any more,

Rama, who dwells in the hearts of good
people,

even as the Age of Kali is starting,
people are driven to evil deeds
again and again, with no respect
for parents and preceptors.

Gloss

As part of his moral preoccupation, Tyagaraja feels that so early in the Age of Kali, people have forgotten their values and obligations to the family and the society. Their lack of respect for parents and teachers particularly bothers him. Without the basic decencies of conduct, there is no such thing as devotion or any other lofty endeavour.

Sudhā mādhurya bhāṣaṇa
Raga *Sindhu Rāmakriya*

p. sudhā mādhurya bhāṣaṇa sudhākar ānana

a. kath āmṛtamuce bahu kālamu
ākali tīri unnānu brōvumu

c. durātmul agu bhū kirātakula
cēra rādanucu sundar ākāra nī
parāyaṇula celimi rā kōru tyāga-
rāja nuta ō parātpara suguṇa

O sweet-spoken Rama,

I am sated by the nectar of your
life story for long,

Shunning the hoodlums
of the land, I have sought
the company of your followers.

Gloss

One way a devotee can progress spiritually is to avoid the company of evil people and join the circle of devout persons. Here Tyagaraja is relating that fact to the Lord, implying that he is ripe for liberation. He must have seen a lot of undesirable characters around him that he mentions them in a number of his songs.

Durātmulu (evil people) and *bhū kirātakulu* (savages of the land) are a harsh criticism of immoral individuals.

Tappakanē vaccunā
Raga *Śuddha Bangāḷā*

p. tappakanē vaccunā
tanuvuku lampaṭa nī kṛpa

a. meppulakai koppulu gala
mēṭi janula jūci bhajana

c. rūkalakai paiki manci
kōkalakai yāhāramunaku
nūkalakai dhyāninciti
tyāgarāja nutuni bhajana

How do I earn your grace,
being attached to the body?

Can I worship you
while I run after the high
and the mighty for vanity?

I prayed only for food and clothing—
can I serve the Lord?

Gloss

The devotee expresses self-doubt in this song. Having spent all his time in worldly pursuits and nourishing his body, he wants to know if he can still qualify for the Lord's grace. An understandable predicament in which most of us find ourselves. And the answer is contained in the song itself: those pursuits are a waste of time. One should shun the world, as Sankara would say (*Aparokṣānubhūti*, 4, *yathaiva kāka viṣṭāyām*), as if it were the droppings of a crow and cultivate total renunciation.

Vaddanē vāru lēru
Raga *Ṣaṇmukhapriya*

p. vadd anē vāru lēru

a. addampu mōmunu jūḍa
nēn anayam angalārcitē jūci

c. kōrikal ilalō divilō
koncem aina lēni nā manasu
dāri teliyu daivamu nīvu sumī
tyāgarāja hṛd bhūṣana ninu vinā

I have no one to commiserate with me,
as I pine to lay eyes on your lovely face.

You are the only one who knows
that I have entirely given up desire
in both worlds. Look kindly on me.

Gloss

In a mood of utter hopelessness coupled with great longing to see the Lord, the devotee narrates his story to the Lord Himself. He says that he has no desire left in this world or the next, and that no one consoles him in his state of mind. For He alone knows his mind. No special devices in the lyric.

Virāja turaga
Raga *Balahamsa*

p. virāja turaga rāja rājēśvara nirāmayuni jēyavē

a. jarādi rōgayuta tanuvucē narādhamulu yēmi sādhinciri

c. nirantaramu sakala viṣaya duhkha
paramparalacē civukaga madilō
duranta kāma madamunu bādhincaga
durmatuḍē tyāgarāja sannuta

O Garuda-riding Lord,
make me whole.

People afflicted by old age and sickness
have achieved nothing.

The evil-minded one attracted to worldly pleasures
Suffers the pangs of lust,
resulting in ceaseless sorrow.

Gloss

It's strange that Tyagaraja would write a whole lyric on the single subject of physical health, when the body itself is regarded as not part of the spiritual equation. Apparently, he took care of his own body very well in real life. It makes sense on every level to think that he is talking about mental and spiritual health as well in the pursuit of *jñāna.*

Yajñādulu sukham anuvāriki
Raga *Jayamanōhari*

p. yajñ ādulu sukham anu vāriki samul-
ajñānulu galarā ō manasā

a. sujñāna daridra paramparul-
asura cittulu jīv ātma himsa gala

c. bahu janmambula vāsana yutulai
ahi viṣa sama viṣay ākṛṣṭulai
bahir ānanulai tyāgarāju
bhajiyincu śrī rāmuni teliyaka

No one is as ignorant as someone
who claims that works lead to liberation.

Such folks lack basic knowledge
of the Spirit and hurt life

in the name of religion.

Blinded by the sins of past lives,
addicted to sense distractions,
and deluded by the world,
they know nothing about Sri Rama.

Gloss

In this very important lyric, we understand the underlying spiritual basis of Tyagaraja's musical compositions. *Every* song of his has a message that is directly related to the Supreme, even the fairly innocuous ones. To say that he was just a bhakta would be highly misleading. To say that he was just a musician would be a half-truth. He was a saint through and through, which was why Paramahamsa Brahmanandendra was reluctant to initiate him into *sannyasa*. His music was divine. His songs were replete with knowledge of Brahman. His *goal* was Brahman. He compares the performers of rituals mercilessly with demons and their philosophy with the venom of a snake.

SECTION II

MOODS

This is the largest of the three sections encompassing Tyagaraja's lyrics addressing Rama in every mood that he could think of: angry, reproachful, apologetic, critical, frivolous, sensuous, and desperate, but not for one moment straying from the strictest devotion to Him. The changing moods are meant to represent the attitudes of people in general who can redeem themselves through surrender to God, *śaraṇāgati.*

Abhimānam ennaḍu kalgurā
Raga *Kannaḍa*

p. abhimānam ennaḍu kalgurā
anāthuḍ aina nādupai nīku

a. aparādhamul anni mannimpumayya
abhirāma paṭṭābhi rāma nā yandu

c. kanna talliyu kanna taṇḍriyu
anniyu nīvē yani namma lēdā
ninu vinā gati nākevaru lērē
nannu brōvu tyāgarāja vinuta

When will you show mercy
to this destitute?

Forgive me my transgressions,
seeing that you are my father,
mother and all, without whom
I have nowhere to turn.

Gloss
There's some question as to whether the song belongs to the Tyagaraja canon. Regardless, its message and heart-rending supplication to the Lord undoubtedly match the rest of his work.

Āḍa mōḍi galadē
Raga *Cārukēśi*

p. āḍa mōḍi galadē rāmayya māṭa(l)

a. tōḍu nīḍa nīvē yanucunu bhakti
kūḍina pādamu paṭṭina nātō māṭa(l)

c. caduvul anni telisi śankar āṃśuḍai
sadayuḍ āśuga sambhavuḍu mrokka
kadalu tammuni palka jēsitivi gākanu
tyāgarāju āḍina māṭa(l)

Why do you avoid talking to me,

though I bow to you as the One
who is my all, with great devotion?

When at least the learned Hanuman,
of Siva's lineage, wanted to converse,
you made your brother respond.

Why just be hard on me?

Gloss

The saint wonders out loud why Rama doesn't want to talk to him at least indirectly, as he did with Hanuman through Lakshmana during their first encounter when Hanuman wanted to ascertain who the two wanderers were. This is his way of needling the Lord to engage in conversation with him. The two prominent consonantal sounds employed in the service of the lyric are *ḍ* and *d.* Also, while the first sound occurs in predominantly dissyllabic words following long vowels (*āḍa, mōḍi, tōḍu, nīḍa),* the second one appears in *caduvu(lu), sadayu(ḍu), kadalu.* To appreciate a conscious lyricist, we have to assume that every single usage and variation thereof is significant and is designed to create a particular effect, and alter the tempo of the song and the impact on the audience.

Ānanda sāgaram īdani
Raga *Garuḍadhvani*

p. ānanda sāgaram īdani dēhamu
bhū bhāramu rāma

a. śrī nāyak ākhila naigam āśrita
sangīta jñānam anu

c. śrī viśva nātha śrī kānta vidhulu
pāvana mūrtul upāsinca lēdā
bhāvinci rāga layādula
bhajiyincē śrī tyāgarāja nuta

The human body
that's not soaking in divine happiness
derived from the knowledge of music

is so much deadwood.

Haven't Brahma, Vishnu, and Śiva
extolled the virtues of music
that's emanated from the Vedas?
Tyagaraja revered those sentiments,
notes and rhythms.

Gloss
This is one of many compositions in which the composer explicitly sings the praises of the art and science of music. Note that he lends credence to our assertion that *bhāva* (sentiment, purport, feeling) precedes *raga* and *laya* in a *geya (Lyric)*.

Ataḍē dhanyuḍurā ō manasā
Raga *Kāpi*

p. ataḍē dhanyuḍurā ō manasā

a. satata yāna suta dhṛtam aina sītā
pati pāda yugamula satatamu smariyincu

c1. venuka tīka tana manasu ranjillaga
ghanam aina nāma kīrtana paruḍ ainaṭṭi

c2. tumburu vale tana tambura paṭṭi
day āmbudhi sannidhānambuna naṭiyincu

c3. sāyaku sujanula bāyaka tānu
nupāyamunanu proddu hāyiga gaḍipina

c4. ullapu tāpamu calla jēsi anni
kallalani yenci sallāpamuna nunḍu

c5. kari varaduni tatvam eruganu marigincu
ari ṣaḍ vargamulandu parava lēka tirugu

c6. ārtini mariyu pravṛttini tolagincē
kīrti kalgina rāma mūrtini nera nammu

c7. kalagani nija vipra kulamuna janminci
niluvaramagu mukti phalamunu jēkonna

c8. karma niṣṭhuḍaina dharma śīluḍaina
śarma rāma nāma marmamu telisina

c9. kāsu vīsamula kōsamu āsatō
vēsamu dharinci mōsamu jendani

c10. andamugā nāmam andaru jēsina

sundara rāmuniyandu lakṣyamu peṭṭu

c11. inni pāṭulaku sarv ōnnatamau sukhamu
munna yanubhavincukonna vāḍ evaḍō

c12. rājasa janulatō tā jata gūḍaka
rājillu śrī tyāgarāja nutuni nammu

He indeed is hallowed, O Mind,

who forever holds in his heart
the feet of Him who is revered by Hanuman
who to his heart's content sings the praises of Him
who like Tumburu prances with his lute in His court
who with good men happily spends all his time
who enjoys peace knowing all this to be an illusion
who shuns the six enemies that veil His true nature
who submits to Rama who dispels pain and misery
who, born lofty, aspires for self-realization
who knows his duty and the power of His name
who is not fooled by those who dissemble for a living
who only trusts to the lovely name of Rama
who in former lives had already enjoyed the bliss
and detached himself from the vainglorious.

Gloss
The lyric lays out all the desirable qualities and experiences of the ideal devotee.

This long song is a tribute to the composer's ability to state the familiar theme of Rama's praise couched in novel vocabulary to produce a series of sound effects through sets of 3 or more words that either rhyme or almost rhyme. In any case, there is always consonance or repetition of the consonant. Examples abound: *satata, dhṛta, Sita, pati; venuka, tana, manasu, ghana;*

tumburu, tambura, dayāmbudhi, etc.

But it's certainly not all sound and fury. Each set of repeated sounds drives home a philosophical, devotional, or spiritual principle in the mind of the committed aspirant, and the accompanying music highlights the intensity of the emotional quotient of their inherent euphony. In short, the choice of sounds and their repetition enhances the impact of the music that wraps up the whole package.

Aṭla palkuduv iṭla
Raga *Aṭhāṇā*

p. aṭla palukuduv iṭla palukuduv-
anduk ēmi sētu rāma

a. toṭlan arbhakulan ūtuvu mari mari
tōcinaṭlu gilluduvu śrī rāma nī(v)

c. jīvula śikṣincaga nērtuvu
ciranjīvulugā jēya nērtuvurā
bhāvam erigi brōtuvu sad bhakta
bhāgadhēya śrī tyāgarāja vinuta

What should I do with you
who speak as you please

You swing the babes in the cradle,
then pinch them, O Rama!

You make people fear you
even as you bless them

you reward their merit
according to their desert.

Gloss

The saint is not confused here, nor is he trying to confuse us. He is just trying to tell us that the Lord's ways could be mysterious. He can appear to be simultaneously testing us and rewarding us. We just need to go along with His game patiently until He blesses us for the steadfastness of our conviction. The lyric can be viewed as indicating a mild reproach of the Lord for his game-playing. Why not just reward us right away for our devotion?

There are the sound effects generated by the conjunct consonants *t, l,* and repetition of *bhāva/bhāga; jīva/ciraṇjīva/jēya.*

Badalika tīra pavvaḷincavē
Raga *Rītigauḷa*

p. baḍalika tīra pavvaḷincavē

a. saḍalani duritamulanu tega kōsi
sārvabhauma sākēta rāma

c. pankaj āsanuni paritāpamu kani
pankaj āpta kula pativai velasi
pankajākṣitō vanamunak ēgi
jinkanu vadhiyinci
manku rāvaṇuni madamun aṇaci
niśśankuḍagu vibhīṣaṇuniki bangāru
lankan osagi surula brōcina
niṣkaḷanka tyāgarājuni hṛdayamuna

Relax and rest up, O Lord of Lords,
shattering the gravest of my sins.

Aiding Brahma, you became chief of Solar kings,
Going to the forest, you slew the disguised deer,
Killing Ravana, you enthroned Vibhishana
And shielded the gods.

Repose in the pure heart of Tyagaraja.

Gloss
There may be nothing spectacular about the lyric, except the -*ṅka* rhyme repeated in every line of the last verse. It would be interesting to speculate the impact of this repetition on the audience when properly rendered by a competent performer, exploring the possible rhythmic variations and improvisations.

Bāg āyen ayya
Raga *Candrajyōti*

p. bāg āyen ayya nī māyal entō
brahmak aina koniyāḍa taramā

a. ī gāruḍamunu yonarincucu
nē kād anucu palkuṭayu

c. ala nāḍu kauravulan aṇacam ana
alari dōsam anu naruni jūci pāpa
phalamu nīku tanaku lēd ani cakkaga
pālanamu sēya lēdā tyāgarāja nuta

Good job, even Brahma
can't figure out your scam;
I protest—

You assured Arjuna
who refused to fight his kinsmen
that no sin would attach to him
or yourself—and kept your word!

Gloss
A general favorite of concert singers, the song manipulates Lord Krishna's advice to Arjuna to destroy his enemies in war and no sin would accrue to him. Tyagaraja appears determined to exploit this "loophole" in our philosophy of nonviolence.

Bhuvini dāsuḍ anē
Raga *Śrī Rañjani*

p. bhuvini dāsuḍ anē pērāsacē
bonkul āḍitinā budha manōhara

a. avivēka mānavula gūḍi
aḍḍa drōva tokkitinā brōvavē

c. cāla saukhyamō kaṣṭamō nēnu
jāli jenditinā sari vārilō
pāla muncina nīṭa muncina
padamulē gati tyāgarāja nuta

Claiming to be your follower,
have I ever lied?

Moving with deluded people,
have I swerved from the righteous path?

Rain or shine, I haven't complained,
no matter what, I won't let go of your feet.

Gloss

Another plaintive supplication from the devotee explaining unasked that he had been a good person and hence deserves to be helped by the Lord. Note the repeated sound sequences: *bhuvi-bonku-budha; aviveka-aḍḍa (drōva)* (assonance, vowel repetition); *cāla-jāli-pāla* (rhyme). This device here is meant to emphasize the devotee's conviction that he did everything right and is therefore entitled to the Lord's protection. And, tangentially, the composer criticizes those devotees who cash in on their "reputation" as devotees.

Calam ēlarā
Raga *Mārga Hidōḷam*

p. calam ēlarā sākēta rāma

a. valaci bhakti mārgamu tōnu ninnu
varṇincucunna nātō

c. endu pōdu nēnēmi sēyudunu
eccōṭa nē mora peṭṭudunu
dandanalatō poddu pōvalenā
tāḷa jālarā tyāgarāja nuta

Why are you playing games with me

when I praise you like a true devotee?

Where would I go to file
my grievance? Should I spend my day in
turmoil? Can't take
your antics any more.

Gloss

Just a desperate devotee praying earnestly for the Lord's grace. The greater the longing, the more focused the devotee becomes and further prayer is triggered on his part. The longing is an indication of the increasing ripeness of the devotee to receive His grace.

Eduṭa nilicitē nīdu
Raga *Śankarābharaṇam*

p. eduṭa nilicitē nīdu sommul ēmi pōvurā

a. nuduṭi vrāta kāni maṭṭu mīranu nā taramu telisi mōsa pōdunā

c1. sarāsariga jūturā nādu yavasarāla teliyumu varāl aḍuga
jālarā sakala dēva rāya manavi vinar āgha hara sundar ākāra nā

c2. vidēhajā ramaṇa dēva brōvaga nidē samayam anya dēvatala
vēḍadē manasu teliyad ēmi rāghava idēṭi śauryamu padē padē nā

c3. tarāna dorakani parāku nā yeḍanu rāma jēsitē surāsurulu
metturā yipuḍu yī harāmi tanam ēlarā bhakta tyāgarāja nuta nā

What do you lose if you show yourself to me?

I won't be fooled into forgetting my limitations.

Neither will I exceed my needs when I ask for favours.

Sita's consort, it's time to show your grace,
I won't seek favours from other gods,
Don't you know what I want?

The gods won't like your showing
such unusual indifference.
Why this mischief now?

Gloss
Tyagaraja challenges the Lord to appear before him because, after all, it's His job to know what the devotee wants. Trisyllabic words chosen to reinforce his request, with the repeated long *r* include *tarāna, parāku,* and *harāmi. R* and *d* sounds also abound in the first part of the lyric.

Ē dāri sancarinturā
Raga *Śrutirañjani*

p. ē dāri sancarinturā yika palkarā

a. śrīd ādi madhyānta rahita
sītā samēta guṇākara nē(n)

c. anni tān anu mārgamuna canaga
nannu vīḍanu bhāram ani yāḍedavu
tannu brōvu dāsa varadā yanṭē
dvaituḍ anedavu tyāgarāja nuta

Which should be my path,
dvaita or advaita?

If I say I am all,
I am guilty of egotism;
if I ask you to save me,
I am setting us apart!

Gloss
In this brief composition, Tyagaraja asks God a trick question, whether he should be a monist or a dualist in order to be liberated. Either approach entails a problem: nondualists may end up being egotists thinking they are nondifferent from the Almighty, whereas dualists can never hope to be united with Him. He however knows the answer: no matter how you approach the Lord, you are saved. Intense devotion will lead one to Self-realization, where there are no questions or a questioner. The saint is telling us here that it is idle to debate the relative merits of *dvaita* and *advaita* because, if one cultivates devotion to the Lord, one is sure to be saved anyway, regardless of one's approach. In other words, bhakti is the simplest and most direct way to Self-Realization.

Ē nāṭi nōmu
Raga *Bhairavi*

p. ē nāṭi nōmu phalamō
ē dāna balamō

a. śrī nātha brahmak ainanu nīdu
sēva dorukunā tanaku kaluguṭa

c1. nēnu kōrina kōrkel ellanu
nēḍu tanaku neravērenu
bhānu vamśa tilaka nā pāli
bhāgyamā sajjana yōgyamā tana(k)

c2. nīdu dāpu nīdu prāpu dorikenu
nijamugā nē nī somm aitini
ādi dēva prāṇa nātha
nād ankamandu nunci pūjinca

c3. sundarēśa suguṇa bṛnda daśaratha
nandan āravinda nayana pāvana
andagāḍa tyāgarāja nuta sukham-
anubhavinca dorikerā bhaḷi tana(k)

It must be my vows from a past life
or acts of charity that granted me
your worship now.

All my wishes are fulfilled,
thanks to my good fortune,
I have earned your company
and placed you on my lap to adore,
I belong to you and rejoice in you.

Gloss
In the popular stage raga *Bhairavi,* Tyagaraja creates magic with this *Prahlāda Bhakti Vijayam* song and celebrates his good fortune. He expresses his happiness in many songs for

being physically close to Rama, offering him every imaginable service. The last verse (not translated here) addressing the Lord by his various attributes employs rhyming vocabulary and appropriate pauses to close with a heightened effect on the audience.

Ē tāvuna nērcitivō
Raga *Yadukula Kāmbhōji*

p. ē tāvuna nērcitivō rāma
enduk inta gāsī

a. sītā lakṣmaṇa bharata ripughna
vātātmajulatō nāḍē nāṭakamē

c. ālu vajrāla sommul aḍigirō
anujulu talli tanḍrul annam aḍigirō
śīlulaina vara bhaktulu pilicirō
cira kālamu tyāgarāja nuta nīvu

Where did you learn to play tricks
and why all the deviousness, Rama?

Surely, this is a show you put on
with Sita, Lakshmana, Bharata,
Satrughna, and Hanuman.

You have not incarnated
to buy jewellery for Sita
or to feed your family,
but in response to
petitions from pious devotees.

Gloss
Sincere prayers from devotees take many forms. Here Tyagaraja is sure that the Lord took the trouble of incarnating in the world *and* learning how to playact, not to fulfill the material wants of his family but to relieve the suffering of His sincere devotees.

Ētāvunarā nilakaḍa
Raga *Kalyāṇi*

p. ē tāvunarā nilakaḍa nīku
enci jūḍa nagapaḍavu

a. sītā gaurī vāgīśvari yanu
śrī rūpamul andā gōvinda

c. bhū kamal ārk ānila nabhamul andā
lōka kōṭul andā
śrī karuḍagu tyāgarāja kar ārcita
śiva mādhava brahm ādula yandā

Where do you reside, Govinda,
you aren't seen anywhere!

Are you merged in the forms of
Sita, Gauri, or Sarasvati?

Or immanent in the elements,
the myriad worlds,
or morphed as the Trinity?

Gloss

This is a rhetorical way of saying that the Lord is omnipresent and all-pervasive. The lyricist has no doubt that He exists everywhere, if only we know how to see him. This mindset is important for any devotee who longs to see the physical form of Him who *has* no physical form.

Ēl āvatāram ettukoṇṭivi

Raga *Mukhāri*

p. ēl āvatāram ettukoṇṭivi
ēmi kāraṇamu rāmuḍai

a. ālamu sēyuṭakā ayōdhya
pālana sēyuṭakā ō rāghava

c. yōgulu jūcuṭ andukā bhava
rōgula brōcuṭ andukā śata
rāga ratna mālikalu racincina tyāga-
rājuku varam osaguṭ andukā

Why did you incarnate as Rama,

Was it to fight mighty wars
or to govern the kingdom of Ayodhya?

Was it to appear in human form before yogis,
to cure the mighty disease called samsara,
or to bless Tyagaraja,
the creator of garlands of lyrics on Rama?

Gloss

This is very similar to the song before, *ē tāvuna nērcitivō,* where the composer questions Rama about His real mission here on Earth. The answers then were somewhat different from those suggested here in tone but are very similar in substance. There Rama saves the sages, whereas He has a single client here, Tyagaraja, who praises Him in a thousand different ways.

Ēla nī daya
Raga *Aṭhāṇa*

p. ēla nī daya rādu parāku jēsē vēḷa samayamu kādu

a. bāla kanakamaya cēla sujana paripāla śrī ramā lōla vidhṛta śara
jāla śubhada karuṇ ālavāla ghana nīla navya vana mālik ābharaṇa

c1. rārā dēv ādi dēva rārā mahānubhāva rārā rājīva nētra raghu vara putra
sāratara sudhā pūra hṛdaya parivāra jaladhi gambhīra danuja
samhāra madana sukumāra budha jana vihāra sakala śruti sāra nādupai

c2. rājādhi rāja muni pūjita pāda ravi rāja lōcana śaraṇya ati lāvaṇya
rāja dhara nuta virāja turaga sura rāja vandita pad āja janaka dina
rāja kōṭi sama tēja danuja gaja rāja nicaya mṛga rāja jalaja mukha

c3. yāga rakṣaṇa parama bhāgavat ārcita yōgīndra suhṛd bhāvit ādyanta rahita

nāga śayana vara nāga varada punnāga suma dhara
sad āgha mōcana
sadā gatija dhṛta pad āgam ānta cara rāga rahita śrī
tyāgarāja nuta

Why are you unkind to me?
This is no time to abandon me.

You who wear the gilded garments,
saviour of the pure, Consort of Lakshmi,
bestower of auspicious gifts,
the seat of compassion, the king of kings,

worshipped by the sages, exceedingly
charming,
and effulgent as a thousand suns,
protector of sacrifices, without
beginning, middle, or end,
and utterly without attachment.

Gloss

This stage-tested perennial favorite of audiences over the centuries is once again a catalog of the Lord's traits that does not have any semantic content. So we have just paraphrased it, leaving out the full detail. The composition's enduring popularity derives from the regularly occurring rhymes in each of the segments: *-l-* in the *anupallavi*, *-r-* in the first verse, *-j-* in the second, and *g* in the third. More than the rhymes themselves, the closely placed, rhythmically controlled, short phrases shape the final impact of the *kṛti*. The song has many long Sanskrit compounds.

Ēm ānat iccēvō
Raga *Śahāna*

p. ēm ānat iccēvō ēm encināvō

a. nā māṭalu vinavō rāma nā tala vrāl ēmō

c. yaśam āyuvu sad bhaktiyu ēkānta cittamu
suśarīram osangē bhāsura tyāgarāja nuta

What's your instruction to me,
what do you have in mind for me?

Won't you listen to me,
is this my destiny?

O Rama, you who grant fame,
long life, devotion, and
a stable mind and body.

Gloss
Sometimes, the devotee is confused how he should proceed with his services to the Lord, so he asks the Lord Himself for guidance. In the meantime, he feels that he is destined to fail and that his dear Lord is turning a deaf ear to his entreaties. Yet he knows that the Lord alone is capable of granting him the necessary inner strength and stamina. Even in a simple song like this, Tyagaraja does not forget his goal of Self-Realization.

Ēm ani māṭāḍitivō
Raga *Toḍi*

p. ēm ani māṭāḍitivō rāma
evari manasu ē vidhamō telisi

a. māma maradulu anujulu talli tanḍrulu
bhāmalu parijanulu svavaśam auṭak (ēmani)

c. rājulu munulu sur āsurulu vara
dig rājulu mari śūrulu śaśi dhara dina
rājulu lōpaḍi naḍavanu tyāga-
rāja vinuta naya bhayamuga mudduga

Amazing how you spoke with people,
knowing what exactly each wanted to hear—

kinsfolk, parents, servants,
kings, sages, gods, the sun and the moon—

softly, sweetly, harshly,
so they'd do your bidding.

Gloss

This is a form of praise of Sri Rama by Tyagaraja, who is amazed by the psychological savvy and the interpersonal dynamics displayed by Him in His conversations with different classes of people. Tyagaraja believes that only a super smart entity like Rama alone could pull off all the successful interactions that he had with widely disparate groups of people. To the devotee, even the smallest accomplishments on the part of his role model appear magnificent.

Ēmi nēramu nannu
Raga *Śankarābharaṇam*

p. ēmi nēramu nannu brōva
enta bhāramu nā valla

a. sāmaja rāja varaduḍani munu
lasat kīrti kalga lēdā nāpai

c. dīna bandhuvani dēva dēvuḍ-
asamāna ghanuḍani dharm ātmuḍ anucunu
jñāna dhanulu guṇa gānamu sēya
birāna jūḍavu tyāgarāj ārcita nāpai

What have I done wrong,
how hard is it to save me?

You saved the distressed elephant
and earned much praise
as the friend of the lowly,
the god of gods, the unequaled,
the mighty and the virtuous One.

Can't you look after me?

Gloss
This is a supplication from an anguished devotee to the Lord, who has been known as the friend of the lowly. He simply asks Him how hard it would be to save a humble man in distress, when He had no problem rescuing the mighty pachyderm. The lyric highlights the humility of the supplicant. Repetitive *-n-* in the last verse is the dominant sound.

In the second last line, Tyagaraja interjects the phrase *jñāna dhanulu,* seekers endowed with Self-Knowledge, whose authority is beyond question, superior to ordinary devotees. Note the persistent reference to *jñāna* alongside of bhakti, hinting that that is the ultimate goal.

Endu bāyerā daya
Raga *Dhanyāsi*

p. endu bāyerā daya
ina kula tilakā daya

c1. indu vadana kunda radana
mandara dhara nī daya

c2. śānta bhūṣa bhakta pōṣa
śaraṇu śēṣa śāyi

c3. śrita śaraṇya sura varēṇya
kṛta supuṇya dhanya daya

c4. nāga rāja dhara nut āja
tyāgarāja varadā daya

O Scion of the Solar Race!

What happened to your grace,
That disappeared without a trace?

O Lotus-faced One, etc.

Gloss

There can be no simpler lyric than this. Tyagaraja has deftly woven a 10-line lyric around the single query about the perceived lack of the Lord's compassion. He accomplished this feat by the use of a long list of rhyming noun phrases. It would seem that the composer's main intention is to enumerate the Lord's attributes, using the simple question as a ruse. He just enjoys singing the glory of Rama under the pretext of a query.

Enduk ī calamu
Raga *Śankarābharaṇam*

p. enduk ī calamu nēn evaritō telpudu

a. kandarpa janaka nīk ē
kānta ceppenō hari hari

c1. kausalya ceppenō nīkē sammati lēdō
ahalya ceppenō nann ādarinca lēvō

c2. kabarī bhāriṇi sītā kānta ceppenō lēka
śabari ceppenō nīdu śāntam endu pōye

c3. bālayau svayamprabha ceppenō
tāḷa nā taramā śrī tyāgarājunipai

Why are you wishy-washy
and to whom shall I complain?

Which woman is squealing on me,
O Hari? Kausalya, Ahalya, Sita,
Śabari, or the youthful Svayamprabha?
Maybe you are reluctant yourself
and don't care to comfort me.

How can I handle it? Where's your aplomb?

Gloss
Sri Rāma is impervious to female charm and dulcet voice. Tyagaraja turns this around to taunt Him and tries to show that after all He too can be swayed by a woman's baseless insinuations. He is quick to assume, without evidence, that it is a woman who has turned Rama's mind against him, when it's

not his own fate. However, this is just convention and cannot be the saint's conviction or the result of his misogyny. After all, he relented and blessed the talented dancer Kamalamba wholeheartedly. While his disgust of evil people is organic, his aversion to women is merely conventional.

Enduku nirdaya evaru
Raga *Hari Kāmbhoji*

p. enduku nirdaya evar unnārurā

a. indunibh ānana ina kula candana

c1. parama pāvana parimaḷ āpaghana

c2. nē para dēśi bāpavē gānī

c3. uḍata bhakti kani ubbatillaga lēdā

c4. satrula mitrula samamugā jūcē

c5. dharalō nīvai tyāgarāju pai

Why are you hard on me,
knowing I have no one to turn to?

I am a stranger, please help—
weren't you pleased with the squirrel
that contributed its mite?

You love all alike.

You are the refuge of this world.

Gloss
Tyagaraja quizzes the Lord why He was so hard-hearted toward him, knowing that he depended on Him totally. As always, there are the rhymes and alliterations. Earnestly, he reminds the Lord that no creature is insignificant to Him and no service goes unrewarded. Simple as the sentiment is, it's the sincerity that counts. With Tyagaraja, the simpler the appeal is, the stronger its impact on the audience because of the use of homely analogies and well-chosen words.

Endunḍi veḍalitivō
Raga *Darbār*

p. endunḍi veḍalitivō ēvūrō nē teliya ipuḍaina telupavayya

a. anda candamu vērai naḍatal ella tri guṇ ātītamai yunnadē kāni śrī rāma

c. ciṭukanṭē aparādha cayamula tagilincē śiva lōkamu kādu
vaṭu rūpuḍai balini vancinci yaṇacu vāni vaikunṭhamu kādu
viṭa vacanamul āḍi śiramu trumpa baḍḍa vidhi lōkamu kādu
diṭavu dharmamu satyamu mṛdu bhāṣalu kalugu divya rūpa tyāgarāja vinuta

Śrī Rāma, I never knew your origin—

Your looks and acts are beyond
the three attributes.

You cannot be from the world of Śiva
where minor sins are magnified;
you cannot be from the land of Vishnu
who, in the guise of a dwarf,
destroyed Bali with a ruse;
and no way can you be from the world of
Brahma
who lost a head due to his two-faced talk.

So where can you be from,
who speaks the truth gently,
boldly, and righteously?

Gloss

This song tries to separate Sri Rama's persona from those of the Trinity each of whom appears to have a blemish of His own. It is Tyagaraja's way of glorifying his chosen deity over every other god. Sankara in a *Śivānandalaharī* verse (4) prays to Śiva: "There are thousands of lesser gods that grant minor wishes. I have no use for them, and I don't think of them even in my dreams..."

Rhymes in the song include *endu-anda-canda; ciṭuku-vaṭu-viṭa-diṭavu.* The first set that refers to Rama is mellifluous, while the second characterizing the Trinity is harsh (if you ignore *diṭavu,* 'courage,' that applies to Rama).

Tyagaraja highlights this distinction between Rama and the Trinity through the use of the powerful colloquial expressions *taginlincē* (literally, snap on), *aṇacu* (squish), *trumpa baḍḍa* (snipped off), all of which indicate lack of decorum and ceremony.

Ennaga manasuku rāni
Raga *Nīlāmbari*

p. ennaga manasuku rāni pannaga śāyi sogasu
pannuga kanugonani kannul ēlē
kannul ēlē kanṭi minnul ēlē

c1. mōhamutō nīla vāri vāha kāntini kērina
śrī harini kaṭṭukonani dēham ēlē
dēham ēlē yī gēham ēlē

c2. sarasija malle tuḷasi viruvāji pārijātapu
virulacē pūjincani karamul ēlē
karamul ēlē yī kāpuramul ēlē

c3. mālimitō tyāgarājun ēlina rāma mūrtini
lālinci pogaḍani nālik ēlē
nālik ēlē sutra mālik ēlē

Useless are the eyes and their glimmer
if they can't behold the glory of the Lord
reposing on his serpent-bed;

useless is the form that doesn't lovingly
entwine
the blue-cloud-hued body of Śrī Hari,
as is its provenance;

useless are the hands and homes that do not
worship the Lord with fragrant flowers,
and useless are the tongue and the string of
beads
that do not fondly praise Lord Śrī Rāma.

Gloss

Cast in the form of a series of rhetorical questions, it is standard practice in Telugu poetry to disparage the parts of the body that are not engaged in worship, here used in Tyagaraja's *Prahlāda Bhakti Vijaya.* In a less florid form, Sankara uses the theme in *Śivānandalaharī,* verse 94, employing a figure of speech known as *kramālankāra,* which translates literally as: That's the tongue, they are the eyes, those the hands, and he redeemed that (respectively) praises the Lord, behold Him, worship Him, and meditates on Him. While in translation this is awkward, the Sanskrit original is incredibly beautiful. Also, one may say that the Telugu poet Potana (1450-1510) perfected this kind of statement in his well-known poem in the *Bhāgavata* (7.169), *kamalākṣun arcincu karamulu karamulu.* Tyagaraja, who was well-read in the classics in both Telugu and Sanskrit, could very well have been thinking of this poem when he composed this *kṛti.* For his part, he chose the rhyming question format, -*ēlē* (why) for enhanced effect.

Evari māṭa vinnāvō
Raga *Kāmbhōji*

p. evari māṭa vinnāvō rāvō
indu lēvō bhaḷi bhaḷi

a. avanilōn ārṣēya pauruṣēyam andi
cōdyam eruga lēn ayya

c. bhakta parādhīnuḍ anucu
parama bhāgavatula
vyakta rūpuḍai palikina muccaṭa
yuktam anucun unṭi
śakti gala mahādēvuḍu nīv ani
santōṣamunan unṭi

satta cittuḍ agu tyāgarāja nuta
satya sandhuḍ anukonṭin ilalō

Whose chatter have you listened to
and have not shown up here—
good job!

I mastered the Vedas and the epics,
yet I know not the answer.

I heard that you are partial to devotees
and show yourself to them,
the mighty Lord that keeps His word—
I felt happy.

Gloss

This is just plain reproach, where the devotee rebukes the Lord for not living up to His reputation of showing Himself to His worshipers. But the devotee really praises Him and hopes that He will shed His grace on him.

Evar iccirirā
Raga *Madhyamāvati*

p. evar icciri rā śara cāpamulu nīk ina kulābdhi candra

a. avatarincu vēḷan unḍenō lēka avanik ēgi ārjincitivō śrī rāma

c. okaṭ ēsi padi nūrai veyyai cekapikal āḍi śatrulan aṇacen aṭa
vikaluni kākini brōva trimūrtulu venuka tīsir aṭa

sakala nadī patikai drumakulyula samharincen aṭa
prakaṭa kīrti kalgina kōdaṇḍa pāṇi śrī tyāgarāja vinuta

Scion of the Solar Race,
tell me how you got your bow and quiver—

Did you have them when you were born
or acquire them on Earth?

Seems that a single shaft
from the well-known Kodaṇḍa
multiplied manyfold,
made short work of the enemy;
and destroyed the denizens of Drumakulya
at Varuna's bidding;
the Trinity were powerless
to help the crow wounded by you.

Gloss
One way to praise the deity is to depict some attribute or accessory of His in glorious terms such that the devotee's attention is focused on that deity helping their concentration. The praise is then generalized to cover all His attributes. The major sound effect employed in the song occurs in the *caraṇam* where the cacophonous sound *k* invokes a scene of total destruction by Rama's ubiquitous arrows.

Evvarē rāmayya
Raga *Gāngēyabhūṣaṇi*

p. evvarē rāmayya nī sari

a. ravvaku tāvu lēka sujanulanu
rājiga rakṣincu var (evvarē)

c. paga vāniki sōdaruḍ ani yencaka
bhaktin erigi lankā paṭṭam osagagā
naga dhara sura bhūsura pūjita vara
nāga śayana tyāgarāja vinuta sari

Who matches you
in looking after devotees
without the least hesitation?

You made your enemy's sibling
king of Lanka, never holding it
against him.

Gloss
Rama holds the individual responsible for his deeds and not his kinship to others. The relationship between the Lord and the devotee is highly personal. It has no room for nepotism or animosity. The second last line where short vowels are packed tightly contributes to the fast tempo of the conclusion of the lyric and the sentiment.

Garuḍa gamana
Raga *Gaurīmanōhari*

p. garuḍa gamana vāsudēva
karuṇatōnu brōvu nannu

a. parul anna māṭala tāḷanu
paramātmuḍu parama dayāḷō

c. drupada sutā yibha rājuḍu
dhruva bāluḍu moral iḍa vini
grakkuna veḍalina muccaṭa
grammiti tyāgarāja nuta

O Garuḍa-riding Lord,
take pity on me.

I cannot stand the vile gossip.

I was ecstatic when I heard
how you instantly rescued
Draupadi, Dhruva, and the mighty
elephant in distress.

Gloss

Tyagaraja resorts to reminiscing how the Lord promptly saved some of the supplicants in the past to experience joy rather than feel depressed by people bad-mouthing himself. Rhyming is minimal, but a series of short rhythmic phases in the last verse lend charm to the composition when sung meaningfully.

Idi samayamu rā
Raga *Chāyānāṭa*

p. idi samayamurā

a. vidaḷita kali durmada gaja gamana
modaṭa palkinadi nijamuga jēya

c. kali puruṣuḍu nāṭakamunu kaṭṭa

talacināḍu śrī tyāgarāja nuta
khala matamulanē yāgamulaku
mēkaluga narula jēsi nī daya jūḍa

Scion of the Solar line,
now is the time
to fulfill your promise,
and close the curtains
on Kali's evil play
in which humans are
made to be sacrificial
lambs by perverse sects.

Gloss

Every age has its perversities and aberrations among its fringe groups. Adi Sankaracharya risked his life trying to abolish some of those practices. Mild rhyming with *-l-* is seen in the composition. Tyagaraja wisely leaves the dirty job to Rama. The point is that there's no time in the historical context when absolute calm exists and perfect harmony prevails. Social and religious reformers have to deal with them before they can do their job. The *pallavi* and *anupallavi* are almost entirely made up of short vowels, launching the song on a brisk note, moderating toward the end.

Ilalō praṇatārti
Raga *Aṭhāṇa*

p. ilalō praṇatārti haruḍanucu
pērevar iḍirē śankaruḍani nī(k)

a. talaci karagi cira kālamu padamuna

daṇḍam iḍina nāyeḍa daya lēdāye

c. kara caraṇa yuramu nosalu bhujamulu
dharaṇi sōka mrokkaga lēdā
śaraṇ anucunu moraliḍa lēdā
panca nadīśa tyāgarāja nuta

Whoever said you are the reliever of distress
of those who bow to you?

You have no pity for me
who made obeisances to you.

Have I not prostrated myself
with my hands, feet, chest, forehead,
and shoulders touching the ground,
as prescribed?

Gloss

Tyagaraja notes that it's not correct to describe Siva, known as Panchanadīśa in Tiruvaiyar, as the reliever of the distress of those that bow to Him. For He has not shown him any grace, even though he prostrated before Him in the prescribed fashion touching the ground with his hands and feet, chest, forehead, and shoulders. This kind of prostration is technically called *sāṣṭānga praṇāma,* the eight-limbed obeisance.

Inka yōcan aitē
Raga *Ghaṇṭa*

p. inka yōcan aitē nēnēmi sēyudurā

a. pankajākṣa nī vanṭi parama dayā nidhiki

c1. tīrarāni pōrāye sāreku mēnu sagamāye
nēram ēmō teliyadāye āraḍikika tāḷadāye

c2. śrīpati ennikalu lēni tāpatrayamulan alasiti kāni
pāpa gaṇamul anniyu puruṣuni rūpamai bādhincaga
nī(k)

c3. vāgadhipa vandya ninnē kāni yorula nammani
tyāgarājuni paini bāgāye śrī rāma nī(k)

What can I do if you the kindly Lord
are still debating my fate?

No idea why I am tormented,
what my fault is,
though I lost half my weight,

Countless travails besiege me, and
hordes of misdeeds wrack my human frame.

Yet I trusted only you for better or worse,
Rama.

Gloss

A simple petition from Tyagaraja to Rama urging Him not to tarry any longer but save him from the trammels of worldly life. Is there a shortcoming on his part that drains his strength and subjects him to all sorts of afflictions? This is the song of a desperate devotee who fails to come to the notice of the Lord, despite his sincere appeal.

Inta saukhyam ani
Raga *Kāpi*

p. inta saukhyam ani nē ceppa jāla
entō emō evariki telusunō

a. dānta sītā kānta karuṇā
svānta prēm ādulakē telusunu kāni

c. svara rāga laya sudhā rasam andu
vara rāma nāmam anē kaṇḍa
cakkera miśramu jēsi bhujincē
śankaruniki telusunu tyāgarāja vinuta

It's hard to precisely tell
the extent of the bliss:
who knows—
only those steeped in love for the Lord can.

Like Sankara,
because He adds to his
mix of *svara, raga,* and *laya*
the rock candy of Rama nāma.

Gloss

This is Tyagaraja's unequivocal affirmation that music aids devotion. When Siva chants Rama's name, He makes sure that it is accompanied by flawless music. In other words *sāhitya* is needed to experience the full benefits of *sangīta* which, together, lead the devotee to liberation. This is one of many places where the saint emphasizes the role of the lyric as the principal ingredient in the mix called *mokṣa.* It is the rock candy in the elixir of music.

Kālaharaṇam ēla rā
Raga *Śuddha Sāvēri*

p. kāla haraṇam ēlarā harē sītā rāma

a. kāla haraṇam ēla suguṇa
jāla karuṇ ālavāla

c1. cuṭṭi cuṭṭi pakṣul ella
ceṭṭu vedaku rīti bhuvini
puṭṭaganē nī padamulu
paṭṭukonna nannu brōva

c2. poḍavuna yent āḍukonna
bhūmini tyāgambu rīti
kaḍu velasi yunna nīvu
gāka yevaru nannu brōva

c3. dina dinamunu tirigi tirigi
dikku lēka śaraṇu jocci
tanuvu dhanamu nīdē yanṭi
tyāgarāja vinuta rāma

Why wait to show your mercy to me, when,
since my birth, I sought refuge in you,
just like the birds that locate their tree
by flying around in the woods?

Nothing like surrender on earth,
after all the praises are done,
since no one else can save me.

Wandering through
the livelong day,
and finding no other shelter, I

offer myself and my all to you.

Gloss
Tyagaraja says that surrender is the easiest part of bhakti because, when all is said and done, you are left with no other alternative than to lay yourself at the feet of the Lord for Him to do with you as He pleases. So why not surrender right from the start?

Kaḷala nērcinā
Raga *Dīpakam*

p. kaḷala nērcinā munu jēsinadi
gāka yēmi aravai nālugu

a. kalimi lēmulaku kāraṇambu nīvē
karuṇa jūḍavē kaḍupu korakē

c. kōri nūvula koṇḍa tīsi singara muni
kūrmi bhujincenā vairi tammuḍu
sāram aina rangani yillu jērcenā
sarasa tyāgarāja vinuta brōvavē

Accomplished though in all sixty-four arts,
one's fortunes are doled out by you,
please be gracious to us.

Sage Singari couldn't eat
the sesame heap when proffered,
nor could Vibhishana take
Ranganatha all the way to Lanka.

Gloss
Tyagaraja always exemplifies his statements with suitable instances from the epics and scriptures, even if we may not be able to track some of them down. In fact, it's part of his lyrical technique, that makes his compositions memorable. The devotee's faith in the Lord's omnipotence is instantly strengthened.

Kaligiyunṭē kadā
Raga *Kīravāṇi*

p. kaligi yunṭē kadā kalgunu
kāmita phala dāyaka

a. kalini yingitam erugaka ninn āḍukonṭi
calamu cēyaka nā talanu cakkani vrāta

c. bhāgavat āgrēsarul agu nārada
prahlāda parāśara rāmadāsulu
bāguga śrī raghurāmuni padamula
bhakti jēsina rīti tyāgarājunik ipuḍu

Only if we are destined to,
will our wishes be fulfilled;

Or one should cultivate devotion
to the Lord like the renowned
Prahlāda, Parāśara, and Rāmadās.

Not knowing this truth,
I pointed my finger at you!

Gloss

In this song, Tyagaraja implies that, even if you are not destined to achieve something, you can achieve it through great devotion to the Lord. In other words, supreme devotion can override so-called fate. It is meaningless to blame Him for your shortcomings or lack of effort. He asks elsewhere, "*grahabalam emi, rāmuni yanugraham unna,*" what can the planets do if you are protected by Rama?

Kanna taṇḍri nāpai
Raga *Dēvamanōhari*

p. kanna taṇḍri nāpai
karuṇa mānakē gāsi tāḷanē

a. ninna sēyu panulu nēḍu gāka
vērenna lēd anucu vēmārulaku

c. eduru tānanē ingitamb erigi
cedaranīka panc ēndriyam aṇaci
vadala lēni dhairyaśāli kādani
madana kōṭi rūpa tryāgarāja nuta

Father, don't abandon me,
and hold back your compassion.

I do not give up my routine
from day to day, I am steadfast.

Knowing that you are my refuge,
I still cannot subdue my senses
nor can I walk away from you.

Gloss
This composition seems to indicate that the devotee, who is convinced that the Lord is his goal, is nevertheless unable to control his senses. He cannot give up his goal of reaching Him, either, because He is everywhere and cannot be evaded.

Kaṇṭa jūḍumī
Raga *Vācaspati*

p. kaṇṭa jūḍumī oka pāri krē

a. banṭuḍai velayu bāgu kāni tappu
taṇṭal ella mānukonna nannu krē

c. ala nāḍu saumitri pāda sēva
celarēgi cēyu vēḷa sītatō
palki jūcin anta pulak ānkituḍai
paraginayaṭu tyāgarājuni krē

Look at me sideways once—

As your follower, I have given up
all my sinful ways.

When Lakshmana eagerly
massaged your feet, you glanced
approvingly at him while talking to Sita
and made his body tingle.

Gloss
In his eagerness to attract the attention of his Lord, Tyagaraja is willing to settle for a quick side glance that can give him goose

bumps, just like the one that Lakshmana earned from Him. Just as the Lord is satisfied with a leaf, a flower, a fruit, or even a spoonful of water (*patram, puṣpam, phalam, tōyam),* the devotee is thrilled if the Lord but looks at him briefly.

Kanulu tākani
Raga *Kalyāṇa Vasanta*

p. kanulu tākani para kāntala
manas eṭulō rāma

a. nana bōṇulapai nēram ana
nōrēmi rāma

c1. ghōra bhūta patini jūci
dārukāraṇya satulu
mēra mīri bhuvini
yapadūru kalga jēsirē

c2. mana mōhan ānanda
mada cakōra nayana kunda
radana candra vadana
sundar ānga tyāgarāja vinuta

What thoughts reside in the minds
of young women
is hard to know, O beautiful, moon-faced
Rama.

The wives of the sages of Daruka
themselves fell a prey to the fierce
Lord of ghosts and brought
disrepute to their husbands.

Gloss

Somewhat out of context, maybe, Tyagaraja tries to understand the workings of young women's minds. Even the wives of the sages of Daruka were momentarily attracted to the fearsome Lord of ghosts, Śiva. Question is, is it the young women's fault? It is interesting that Tyagaraja now seems to imply that they are merely victims of circumstances and are blinded by love—a rare show of empathy from the stern saint!

Kāru vēlpulu
Raga *Kalyāṇi*

p. kāru vēlpulu nīku sari

a. kāruku jilakara
sambāk antaram ainaṭṭu kāni

c1. diviṭiki dīpamu rīti
kāvēṭiki kāluvala rīti

c2. tammi vairiki tārakala rīti
kamma viltuniki kānti narula rīti kāni

c3. sāgaramunaku sarassu rīti
tyāgarāja vinuta dharalō nīku sari

Other gods are no match for you—
they differ from you
like coarse grain from fine rice,
a torch from a lantern,
a ditch from the Kaveri,
the stars from the moon,
an ordinary man from the God of Love,

and the lake from the ocean.

Gloss
The composer is never tired of comparing ordinary gods with Rama, if only to feel good that they are nowhere near Him in any respect. This helps him maintain his focus on the deity and his mind in a mood of eternal joy. *K* is the dominant sound in the song. When you read lyrics like this, you can clearly see where Tyagaraja is headed with his *sāhitya.*

Kārubāru sēyuvāru
Raga *Mukhāri*

p. kārubāru sēyu vāru
galarē nīvale sākēta nagarini

a. ūrivāru dēśa janula vara
munul uppongucunu bhāvukul ayyē

c. nelaku mūḍu vānal akhila vidyala
nērpu kaligi dīrghāyuvu kaligi
calamu garva rahitulu gālēdā
sādhu tyāgarāja vinuta rāma

Who can rule Saketa like you—

Where the citizens and sages
enjoy uninterrupted happiness,
with thrice-monthly showers,
skilled in all the arts, long-lived,
yet free from conceit and hubris.

Gloss
The lyricist praises each of the admirable qualities of his Lord by turns, this one highlighting His governance of the City of Ayodhya. One way we can tell He is a great administrator is that the citizens are all happy with crops never failing and with the best education available. Though normally that level of satisfaction engenders a certain amount of hotheadedness, that doesn't happen in Rama's city.

Karuṇā samudra
Raga *Dēvagāndhāri*

p. karuṇā samudra nanu
kāvavē śrī rāma bhadra

a. śaraṇāgata hṛcchidra
śamana nirjita nidra

b. nā pāpamu nātōn unṭē
śrīpa nī biruduk ēmi bratuku
ē pāpula śāpamō
endukī calamu tyāgarāja nuta

Redeem me from my sins, Merciful Rama,
Comforter of forlorn hearts.

If I am not redeemed,
think what happens to your reputation;
I must be cursed by some sinner,
or why would you hesitate?

Gloss
One of the devotee's tricks to qualify for the Lord's grace is blackmail. By reminding Him that, if He doesn't save him instantly, His reputation would go down the drain. This is one of many such lyrics composed by Tyagaraja, which is an indication of his closeness to Him. Two rhymes are employed, one featuring the *dra* cluster in the first four lines, and the single consonant *p* in the last four. The repeated cluster has the effect of emphasis and the single consonant evokes a sense of resignation on the part of the devotee. In other words, the devotee both demands and despairs as he deals with the Lord, finally just surrendering to Him.

Kaṭṭu jēsināvu
Raga *Aṭhāṇā*

p. kaṭṭu jēsināvu rāma bandu

a. maṭṭu mitamu lēnaṭṭi dēvatā
matamulalō jorabaḍudām anṭē

c. mā matamulanu lalāṭamuna
pitāmahuḍu vrāya lēd anucunu mari mari
kāma madamulaku hitav anucu
niṣkāma tyāgarājuku tōcē

You cast a spell on me, Rama,
I am your bonded slave.

I cannot follow other gods,
whose wayward paths
lead only to endless desires
and arrogance.

Not bound by destiny,
I am attached to you.

Gloss
Another recurring theme in Tyagaraja's lyrics: he places devotion and service to Rama above all other avenues to the attainment of liberation. This is his way of reinforcing his conviction that Rama alone can teach him true knowledge in the long haul.

Koṭi nadulu
Raga *Tōḍi*

p. kōṭi nadulu dhanuṣkōṭilōn unḍaga
ēṭiki tirigedavē ō manasā

a. sūṭiga śyāma sundara mūrtini
māṭi māṭiki jūcē mahā rājulaku

c. ganga nūpurambunanu janincenu
rangani kāvēri kani rājillenu
pongucu śrī raghu nāthuni prēmatō
pogaḍē tyāgarāju manavi vinavē

If you can see the handsome Lord, O Mind,
you will see all the holy rivers at Dhanushkoti
where He ordered the bridge to be built—

Ganga emanated from His feet,
Kaveri was delighted
to have Ranganatha in her sights—
listen to ecstatic Tyagaraja

that sings His praises.

Gloss

This lyric loses a lot of its charm in translation, because the beauty of the original is based on the play on the words *kōṭi* and *Dhanuṣkōṭi,* the *ṭ* rhymes in the first four lines and the *-nga-* rhymes in the last three lines. The point of course is that, when you have Rama firmly planted in your mind, you don't need to look for holy shrines elsewhere, as exemplified by the fact that the sacred waters of the Ganga emanated from Him and Kaveri enjoys His proximity.

Kṣīrasāgara śayana
Raga *Dēvagāndhāri*

p. kṣīra sāgara śayana nannu
cintala peṭṭa valenā rāma

a. vāraṇa rājunu brōvanu vēgamē
vaccinadi vinnānurā rāma

c. nārī maṇiki cīral iccinadi nāḍē nē vinnānurā
dhīruḍau rāmadāsuni bandhamu tīrcinadi vinnānurā
nīrajākṣikai nīradhi dāṭina nī kīrtini vinnānurā
tāraka nāma tyāgarāja nuta dayatōn ēlukōrā rāma

Why do you torment me, Rama,

I heard about how you saved
the king of elephants;
how you saved the modesty
of Draupadi by granting her

an interminable garment;
how you secured the release of
illustrious Ramadas; and
how you crossed the ocean
to rescue your dear consort.

Gloss
We see this theme repeated elsewhere. Tyagaraja just keeps reminding himself and us of the great deeds his Lord Rama has accomplished to make sure that our focus does not waver. Furthermore, it helps reinforce once's conviction that the Lord who rescued so many others from dire straits will also save us just as surely. The purpose of citing examples of the Lord's good deeds is to confirm to one and all that He can always be relied upon.

Kula birudunu
Raga *Dēvamanōhari*

p. kula birudunu brōcukommu rammu

a. ila kala bhū dēva sur ādulak ādhāruḍ agu nī

c. nigam āgama cara nīku nitya mangaḷamu kalgu
vaga sēyaku rāma vandita tyāgarāja

O Rama, fount of all existence,
come and redeem your family name.

Don't tarry, you defender of the Vedas,
Glory be to you!

Gloss

This borders on the devotee blackmailing the Lord that, if He didn't come pronto to take care of him, His reputation would be shattered. Again, a repetitive theme. Note however that the repetitions in Tyagaraja's lyrics are themselves a way of guaranteeing the devotee's focus on the Lord's proximity to himself.

Lāli lāli yani
Raga *Hari Kāmbhōji*

p. lāli lāli yani yūcērā
vanamāli mālimitō jūcērā

c1. dēva dēva yani pilicērā
mahānubhāva bhāvamuna talacērā

c2. rāma rāma yani palikērā
niṣkāma kāma ripu nuta rārā

c3. kōri kōri ninnu kolicērā
māyadāri dāri sad bhajanarā

c4. rāja rāja yani pogaḍērā
tyāgarāja rāja yani mrokkērā

I rock the swing fondly,
singing lullabies.

I call you the god of gods
while praising you in my mind,

I keep saying O Rama,

the One who abandoned desire
and praised by Śiva,

I worship you over and over,
Because that's the only way,

I bow to the emperor of emperors.

Gloss
Here Tyagaraja employs a different rhyme for each couplet, with quickly changing connotations, but enhancing the overall impact on the audience. This is appropriate for a song that graphically represents the back and forth movement of a swing. Every device that he employs adds a special dimension to the purport of his lyrics. Traditional South Indian lullabies start with *lāli lāli.*

Lāli yūgave
Raga *Nīlāmbari*

p. lāli yūgavē mā pāli daivamā

a. lāli yūgavē nunu gāli tinḍi pānpu paini

c. pammina vēḍuka mīra tammulatōnu
kammani viḍem osagu yā janakātmajatōnu
bomma dēvara tanḍri bhūm īśula tōḍanu
sammatamuna tyāgarāja sannuti sēyaga

Rock on that swing, O Lord,

swing on the serpent bed,

Father of Brahma,

to your heart's content
with your brothers
and your consort who
offers you sweet betel chew,
and with the rulers of the world.

Gloss

This lyric is presented here in juxtaposition with the one above to contrast their varying tempos, though they both have the swing theme. The first one is an agglomeration of disparate acts by the devotee, while the second is a single unified act of the Lord swinging away in the company of His near and dear ones. The verse here has the double *m* rhymes in all four lines to give it a unified structure.

Lēmi telpa
Raga *Navanītam*

p. lēmi telpa peddal evvaru lērē

a. ā mahimal ella māni ī mahilō puṭṭirō

c. nī rūpamunu pūni manasu nirmalulai yunḍa lēdā
dhārādharābha śarīra tyāgarāja vinuta

Isn't there anyone to apprise you
of my indigence?

Are they born on Earth without
those powers?

Haven't they obtained identity
with you through their piety,
O cloud-complexioned Rama?

Gloss

The devotee, tired of waiting for the Lord's grace, questions where all of His informants have disappeared without notifying Him of his impecuniosity. They are probably here on Earth but lost the power to communicate with the Lord, or have merged in Him through their intense devotion. So the devotee is left without an intermediary to communicate with the Lord. It is believed that intercession by a competent and trustworthy person is better than direct appeal.

Madilōna yōcana
Raga *Kōlāhalam*

p. madi lōna yōcana puṭṭa lēdā
maha rāja rājeśvarā

a. padi vēsamulalō rāma vēsamu
bahu bāg anucu kōru nannu brōva

c. iṭṭi vēḷa nīdu maṭṭu jūpumani
illālu nītō muccaṭ āḍadō nā
raṭṭu nī manasuk eṭṭu tōcenō
rakṣincuṭaku tyāgarāja nuta

Hasn't it occurred to you,
O King of Kings,
to render help to me?

I chose the Rama incarnation
as the best of the ten.

Hasn't your dear spouse
talked with you about my
predicament?

Gloss
Tyagaraja involves Sita frequently in any tough situation he finds himself in so that she may intercede on his behalf. So, too, here. The emphasis on this situation is aptly delineated by the repetitive double consonant *t.*

Mahima taggincukōvayya
Raga *Ṛṣabhapriya*

p. mahima taggincukōvayya
mahini satya svarūpuḍ anu
mahā rāja rājēśvara nī

a. vihita mārga bhaktulugā mahātmulu
velayaga vina lēdā svakīyam agu

c. paniki rāni panulu jēsi śaraṇ anu
vāri vetalu tīrci brōcitivē
tanivi tīra namminādḍ anucu śrī
tyāgarāja nuta tappul āḍaku

O Ruler of Rulers,
pray come down to my level.

Haven't there been

well-known devotees
who chose the prescribed path?

You also forgave those who sinned
and surrendered to you;
I fully trusted you,
please don't fault me.

Gloss

This interesting little piece is both a prayer and a reproach addressed to Rama. Tyagaraja tells Rama that there were devotees who were great, as also sinners who later surrendered to Him. He requests Him to overlook his faults too, like he did with the latter, and take care of him.

Mākēlarā vicāramu
Raga *Ravicandrika*

p. māk ēlarā vicāramu
maru kanna śrī rāma candra

a. sākēta rāma kumāra
sad bhakta mandāra śrīkara

c. jata kūrci nāṭaka sūtramunu
jagam ella meccaga karamunan iḍi
gati tappaka āḍincedavu sumī
nata tyāgarāja girīśa vinuta

Sri Ramachandra,
we are not worried,
Scion of Saketa, and
benefactor of followers.

You put together this play,
manage its unfoldment,
and ensure that we act
without missing a step.

Gloss

It is a common trope in Indian philosophy that the world is a show, we are all actors in it, and the Lord is the producer and director. In this complicated production with a multitude of actors and scenes, there never happens a single misstep because He takes care of it. He is no ordinary director. In the *Bhagavadgita* (18.61), Krishna says that Isvara who resides in the hearts of people makes them act according to His will just like puppets. In the last verse, the dominant sound is *t* repeated in words with short vowels.

Compare Shakespeare's play *As You Like It,* Act II, Scene VII, lines 138-141:

All the world's a stage,
And all the men and women merely players:
They have their exits and their entrances;
And one man in his time plays many parts...

The European tradition of comparing the world to a theatrical stage and the people to actors may have been borrowed from the East. Our classics routinely made the comparison and took it further naming God as the director and implying that all creation is a make-believe and ephemeral. Sankaracharya says in his Sivanandalahari (66): "You create the universe for your amusement, and the creatures are prey animals to you."

Mānamu lēdā
Raga *Hamīr Kalyāṇi*

p. mānamu lēda tana vāḍ ani abhi

a. kānamurā nī vale nirmōhini
gāna ruci teliyu kuśa lava janaka

c. nī samukhamuna ravi tanayuḍu ninnu
bāsalu palkaga rōsamutō simhāsan ādhipati jēsina nīku
dāsuḍ aina tyāgarāj kar ārcita

Where's your self-esteem,
and concern for your own,
Father of twins Kuśa and Lava,
who enjoys music,
no one's stoic like you.

You made Sugriva king,
though he upbraided you
for failing to keep your word
the first time.

Gloss

Tyagaraja intends in this composition to praise Rama as a completely impartial Lord in helping his devotees, but He goes about it in a reproachful manner, with the help of the Sugriva episode in the *Ramayana*. Having failed to kill Vāli the first time as promised, He was subjected to denunciation by Sugriva, yet Rama was unaffected. The next time when He could tell the two brothers apart, He did slay Vali, and make Sugriva king of the land without holding his censure against Him. Rama's first priority was upholding dharma.

Manasā śrī rāmacandruni
Raga *Īśa Manōhari*

p. manasā śrī rāmacandruni
maravakē ēmarakē

a. munu puṭṭanu puṭṭina mauni kṛtamau
mūḍunnār adhyāyamulu jūcukō

c. sṛṣṭi puṣṭi naṣṭi sēyu panulu
nikṛṣṭam anucunu trimūrtulak osagi
tuṣṭuḍai paragē sad bhakta
manōbhīṣṭamul iccē tyāgarāja nutuni

O Mind,
never ever forget Sri Ramachandra—

Study books three and six
of Valmiki's great work;

He gave the tasks of
creation, sustenance,
and dissolution
to the Trinity as beneath Him,
and kept for Himself
the blessed job of
granting the wishes of the devotees.

Gloss

Tyagaraja puts his mind to work in several different ways, one of which is just to understand how the Lord works, when it's not working in devious ways. When the mind is up to its usual tricks, he severely chastises it. Which is why it has been said that we can't live *with* the mind, and we can't live *without* the mind!

Manavini vinumā marava
Raga *Jayanārāyaṇi*

p. manavini vinumā marava samayamā

a. kanugona kōri duṣkalpana māniti
kanikaramuna ninu pāḍucunna nā

c. parulaku hitam agu bhāvana kāni
ceracu mārgamula cintimpa lēnu
parama dayākara bhakta manōhara
dhar ādhipa kar ārcita tyāgarāju

Kindest Savior,
worshipped by kings,
consider my plea,
and don't ignore me.

Desiring to find you,
I gave up my evil ways,
and am singing your glory now.
I only think of ways to help
others and not hurt.

Gloss
In this and many other compositions, Tyagaraja directly connects self-improvement to good works and good conduct in life. That's the only way to please the Lord and earn His grace. Note, too, that his chosen way of praising the Lord is through

lyric and song. He makes it a point to let the Lord know that he is doing so as part of his penance to redeem himself from any prior misdeeds. Good works lead to a pure mind, pure mind leads to firm devotion, and unwavering devotion leads one to the Godhead—this, in a way, summarizes Tyagaraja's life and work.

Mariyāda kādayya

Raga *Bhairavam*

p. mariyāda kād ayya manupav adēmayya

a. sarivārilō nannu cauka cēyuṭ ella śrī
hari hari nī vanṭi karuṇā nidhiki

c. tana vārul anyulanē tāratamyamunu
ghanuḍ aina dāśarathikē kaladani kīrti kadā
ninu bāya nērani nannu brōvak unḍēdi
dhanada sakhuḍ agu tyāgarāja pūjita

O Sri Hari,

it's not proper for you to neglect me,

it doesn't behove an ocean of mercy
like you to slight me in front of my peers.

It's well-known that Lord Rama,
worshipped by Śiva,
doesn't discriminate against anyone,
take good care of me
who cannot stay away from you.

Gloss

The text as it has come down to us seems somewhat fuzzy, especially in the *caraṇam.* This paraphrase may deviate from the original, in order to make sense out of what's there. The dominant sound is *r,* and the first three lines are constructed such that they produce a soothing effect on the listeners.

Mummūrtulu gumigūdi
Raga *Aṭhāṇa*

p. mummūrtulu gumi gūḍi pogaḍē muccaṭa vinukōrē

a. sammatiga rāju koḍuk anaga vini
samśayamu tīraka śrī rāmuni

c. rōsamutō raghu rāmuni guṇamula
rūḍhiga tama guṇamula naṭu vrāsi
trāsuna niḍa sari nilva lēdani
tyāgarāja nutuḍ evaḍē yanucunu

Not satisfied with the fact
that you are the son of King Daśratha,

the Trinity weigh their traits
against yours in the balance.

Finding they cannot match
their features to yours,
they wonder who
this great personage
worshipped by Tyagaraja is.

Gloss

In yet another twist in his theme of establishing the superiority of Rama, he weighs the entire set of the Trinity's attributes against the traits of the single personage Rama. As expected, the weigh scale proves the inferiority of the Trinity, which makes them wonder who this person that has outweighed them is. A hyperbolic way of praising Rama as being matchless. Tyagaraja's setting in which the Trinity gather in a huddled group to check Rama out is graphic, highlighted by the word *gumi kūḍi,* a colloquial description of a congregation gathered for conspiratorial reasons.

Nannu brōva nīkinta
Raga *Ābhōgi*

p. nannu brōva nīk inta tāmasamā
nā pai nēram ēmi palkumā

a. cinna nāḍē nī celimi kalga kōri
cintimpa lēdā śrī rāma

c. nija dāsa varul agu tammulatō
nīvu bāga puṭṭaga lēdā
gaja rāja rakṣaka tanayulanu
kani penca lēdā tyāgarāja nuta

Why tarry so long to redeem me,
Tell me where I went wrong.

Did I not pine for you
since my early years?

Don't your siblings adore you?

Haven't you sired and raised your sons?

Gloss

Tyagaraja questions the Lord about why it is taking so long for him to experience His grace. His siblings and children have benefited from Him. Though he longed for Him since his childhood, he has not been blessed by Him. By implication, Tyagaraja is demanding that he should be treated as a co-equal member of His family. What's his fault?

Nāṭi māṭa maracitivō
Raga *Dēvakriya*

p. nāṭi māṭa maracitivō ō rāma cinna

a. māṭi māṭiki nāpai mannana jēyucu
ēṭiki yōcana ī bhāgyamu nīd anu

c. taruṇula bāgu nartanamula jūcu vēḷa
caraṇamulu kani karagucu sēvimpa
bharatuni kara cāmaramunu nilpucu
karuṇanu tyāgarāja varaduḍ ani palkina

Don't you recall, Rama,
Your words from my youth,
telling me not to worry,
because I was fortunate?

While the dancers performed
and I was blissfully rubbing your feet,
you paused Bharata's fan
and pointed me to him with approbation.

Gloss

Ardent devotees turn their attention to their deity so powerfully that they feel that they are in the presence of that deity physically. On one such occasion Tyagaraja imagined that Rama pointed him out to his brother Bharata who was also attending on Him, with approval. Tyagaraja repeats this sentiment in many other contexts as well.

Nē pogaḍakunṭē nīkēmi
Raga *Deśīya Tōḍi*

p. nē pogaḍak unṭē nīkēmi kodavō
nī manasu telise kadarā ō rāma

a. prāpu kala śuka sanaka prahlāda nārada
paramēśa rudr ādi bhaktul arcimpaga

c. bhujiyimpa beṭṭa sati budhulu sāmājikulu
bhajiyimpa sōdarulu pavana sūnuḍ aja
biḍauj ādi surul āptul aināru
nīraja nayana śrī tyāgarāja nuta bāluḍ agu

If I, a boy, don't sing your praises,
it's no loss to you.

Eminent devotees like Śuka.
Sanaka, Prahlada, Rudra,
are ready to worship you.

Your Consort, the gods,
and householders feed you;
your brothers and Hanuman
attend on you; Indra and other

celestials keep you company.

Gloss
In his unique way, Tyagaraja admits that Rama has any number of attendants and devotees, even if Tyagaraja does not serve him. Now that doesn't mean he is not going to serve him but, indirectly, the lyricist is asking Rama not to ignore the little boy (himself) who equally deserves His attention. Interesting! You wonder how many different ways the composer can come up with to praise Rama.

Nija marmamulanu telisina
Raga *Umābharaṇam*

p. nija marmamulanu telisina vārini
nīv alayincēd ēmokō rāma

a. aja gaja rakṣaka gaja carm āmbar ādi
daiva bhēdamula līla kalga jēsina nī

c. śruti śāstra purāṇavid ādi
ṣaṇ mata niṣṭhula nāma par ādula
kṣiti patulan kumatulugā jēsina
kṣēma tyāgarāja nuta śrī manōhara

Why do you delude, O Rama, even those
who know your mysterious ways?

You made the Trinity distinct,
you hoodwinked the followers
of the six faiths, masters of the epics,
chanters of your holy name,

and the rulers of the land.

Gloss

The purport of this song is that no one really knows the Lord's mysterious ways, even those who think that they do. A better way of knowing the Lord is to worship Him and surrender to Him wholeheartedly. Tyagaraja is paying a tribute here to the Lord that He is much more than the sum of His parts.

Nī cittamu niścalamu
Raga *Dhanyāsi*

p. nī cittamu niścalamu nirmalamani ninnē namminānu

a. nā cittamu vancana cancalamani nannu
viḍanāḍakumī śrī rāma

c. guruvu cilla ginja guruvē bhramaramu
guruḍē bhāskaruḍu guruḍē bhadruḍu
guruḍē uttama gati guruvu nīvanukoṇṭi
dharanu dāsuni brōva tyāgarāja nuta

I trusted your steadfast mind,
don't forsake my fickle one.

The mentor is like the cleansing nut,
he's the wasp that stings the worm into shape,
he's the brilliant sun that illuminates,
he's auspicious, he is the highest goal.
And that teacher is you.

Gloss
Tyagaraja, like every other saint and prophct, stresses the significance of a spiritual preceptor for the seeker. He reaffirms his commitment to that notion, as the primary requirement for the acquisition of true knowledge.

Nī daya rādā
Raga *Vasanta Bhairavi*

p. nī daya rādā

a. kād anē vār evaru kalyāṇa rāmā

c1. nannu brōcu vār ilanu nāḍē teliya
ina vamśa tilaka nīk inta tāmasamā

c2. anniṭikin adhikāruḍ ani nē pogaḍitē
mannincitē nīdu mahimaku takkuvā

c3. rāma rāma rāma tyāgarāja hṛt sadana
nā madi tallaḍille nyāyamā vēgamē

Won't you show me mercy, Rama?

who stands in the way?

You knew before
that you are the one to save me,
so why the dithering?

Is it beneath you to forgive me
for praising you as the Lord of all?
My mind is unsettled.

Gloss
In an intimate dialog with the Lord, the devotee argues that he deserves His grace soon, because that was understood long back. The fact that he praised Him as all-powerful should not make Him hesitate. Just another way of appealing to the Lord by an impatient devotee on a personal level.

Nīkē teliyakapōtē
Raga *Ānandabhairavi*

p. nīkē teliyakapōtē
nēnēmi sēyudu rā

a. lōkādhāruḍavai nā
lōni prajvalincu jāli

c. end endu jūcina end endu palikina
end endu sēvincina end endu pūjincina
and andu nīv ani tōcuṭ anduku nī
pād āravindamuni dhyānincinad-
enduk ani tyāgarāja sannuta

My endless yearning is for you
and to meditate on your feet,

wherever I look, talk, or worship,
because you pervade the universe.

If this is not known even to you
what should I do?

Gloss

This song claims that the devotee prays anywhere and everywhere because he is convinced that the Lord is omnipresent. The Lord cannot claim that He is not aware of those prayers. Tyagaraja deliberately used this illogicality to highlight the predicament of the devotee. The *caranam* echoes the famous verse in Potana's *Bhagavata,* where Prahlāda explains to his demon father, in answer to his demand to show him Sri Hari, that He is wherever one looks for him and that there is no place where He isn't in a simple Telugu verse: *indu galaḍ andu lēḍani/sandēhamu valadu cakri sarvōpa gatuṇḍ/ endendu vedaki jūcinan/ andandē galaḍu dānavāgraṇi vinṭē.*

Nī sari sāṭi
Raga *Hēmavati*

p. nī sari sāṭi yevaru lēd anucu
niratamu nē nī padamula talaciti

a. dāsuni brōcuṭak arudāye kadā
bhāsalu vērāye bhaḷi bhaḷi

c. aja kumbhaja muni nagaja pat īndrulu
gaja pati khaga phaṇi rāja varēṇyulu
bhajana parulugā velasiri
tyāgarāja vinuta nā manavi vinuṭaku

I always worship your feet
because there's no one like you.

You have no time for this follower,
you no longer talk about me.

You now have the likes of
Brahma, Siva, Indra,
Garuda and the Serpent Sesha,
to sing your glory.

Gloss

The devotee feels that the Lord is adequately entertained without Him paying attention to himself. Hence this is a complaint, along with many similar accusations. Each time, however, there is a complaint, the devotee gets closer to the Lord's feet though the intensity of his longing and the purification of his mind. The concentration of short vowels in the *caraṇam* suddenly accelerates the tempo and catches the audience unawares—a technique that makes them sit up and take notice.

Nī vāḍa nē

Raga *Sāranga*

p. nī vāḍa nē gāna nikhila lōka nidāna
nimiṣam ōrva kalanā

a. dēv ādhi dēva bhū dēva vara pakṣa
rājīvākṣa sādhu jana jīvana sanātana

c. satyambu nityambu samaramuna śauryambu
atyanta prēmambu amita balamu
nity ōtsavambu kala nīku nija dāsuḍ ani
tathyambu palku śrī tyāgarāj ārcita

Am I not your follower,
O Lord of the Universe.
I can't wait for a minute—

Declare me to be so,
you are the Savior, the Ancient One
who only speaks the truth,
is a warrior with endless might,
so merciful,
and is forever festive.

Gloss

Tyagaraja wants to be declared once and for all that he is the Lord's follower. He asks for such an announcement because that designation is not easy to earn. Earning the title of the Lord's follower means that the devotee is liberated through his purified devotion to Him. Invariably, the saint refers to his liberation through his music, which accompanies his inimitable compositions. Note the *-tya-* rhymes in the last verse, that regulate the tempo of the performance.

Nīvē kāni
Raga *Bilahari*

p. nīvē kāni nannevaru kāturură nīrajadaḷanayana

a. kāvalasina kōrikalicci nannu cāla karuṇinci brōcē talli taṇḍrivi

c1. munu mā vamśamuna kalugu peddalu
tapamulanu jēsi yārjincina dhanamu
vinavayya bahu janmamulanu nēnanēka

virula vēla pūjincina phalamu

c2. śaraṇāgata jana pāpa jvalanamunu
śamana jēyu jalapūrita ghanamu
sura muni jana yōgi gaṇamula hṛdayamu
sugṛhamau saccidānanda ghanamu

c3. sāgara śayana nadulalō mēlaina
svarnadī snānambuna kalgu phalamu
tyāgarāju varamani brahmādulaku
satyamu jēsi palkina tārakamu

O Lotus-eyed One,
none other than you can liberate me.

Fulfilling all my wishes,
you nurtured me as a parent.

You are the fruit of the austerities
practiced by my forefathers,
and my worship with thousands of flowers
across myriad lives.

You are the rain-cloud that extinguishes
the fires of sin of those who seek refuge in you,
You are the Bliss sought after by saints and
celestials.

You declared that I've acquired the merit
that comes from a holy bath in the Ganga,
that confers liberation.

Gloss

It appears that Tyagaraja is expressing gratitude to Rama for all that the Lord has granted him, which is a change from his usual tone of complaint. Rhyme and other sound effects are employed.

Ōra jūpu jūcēdi
Raga *Kannaḍa Gauḷa*

p. ōra jūpu jūcēdi nyāyamā
ō ragh ūttama nī vanṭi vāniki

a. nīrajākṣa munu nī dāsulaku
nīk ēṭi vāvulu telpavē

c. mānam incukaina nīku tōca lēka
pōyina vainam ēmi puṇya rūpamā
dīna rakṣ āśrita mānava
santāna gāna lōla tyāgarāja nuta

Is it fair to look askance at me
for one like you, Lord?

What were your followers before
to you, pray tell.

Aren't you a bit embarrassed,
Refuge of the Wretched?

Gloss
Continuing to quiz the Lord about the reasons why He is in no hurry to help him, the saint asks a tough question about His relationship to those whom He had saved before. The implication is that, since they were not His close relatives, either, he too should qualify for His kindness. Very logical,

right? But Tyagaraja in some of these lyrics feels that he is more equal than the others, because he feels that he is the Lord's own. A very effective lyric from that point of view.

Pālintuvō pālimpavō
Raga *Kāntāmaṇi*

p. pālintuvō pālimpavō
bāg aina palku palki nanu

a. ēlāgu ninn āḍukonna
nēram enca pani lēdu nāpaini

c. paramārtham agu nija mārgamunu
vara dēśikunḍ ānat īyagā
paripūrṇamau bhakti mārgamē yani
bhāvincina tyāgarājuni

Won't you show your grace to me
speaking kindly to me?

Never have I spoken ill of you,
no need to find fault with me.

With total reverence have I
accepted your teaching that
devotion to you is true knowledge
that leads to liberation.

Gloss
This is indicative of total surrender on the part of the devotee. He is happy and contented that he wholeheartedly accepted the

teaching of the Lord that bhakti is capable of securing one's release form the cycle of samsara, by inculcating true knowledge in him. Every lyric of Tyagaraja has the single aim of producing the ultimate knowledge in the devotee and securing his liberation, as we have seen.

Palukavēmi nā daivamā

Raga *Pūrṇacandrika*

p. palukavēmi nādaivamā
parulu navvēdi nyāyamā

a. aluga kāraṇam ēmirā rāma
nīv āḍincinaṭlu yāḍina nātō

c. talli tanḍri bhaktin osagi rakṣinciri
takkina vāral entō himsinciri
telisi yūrak unḍēdi yennāḷḷurā
dēv ādhideva tyāgarājunitō

Why are you mum, Rama,
while everyone is mocking me?

Tell me why you are upset with me,
though I indulged your every whim;

My parents taught me bhakti,
but others tormented me,
how long will you ignore it?

Gloss

Tyagaraja seems to think that people in general are mean and thrive by tormenting godly individuals for no reason. He repeats this idea of his in many songs, and uses it as a reason that the Lord should help him. Here the parents raise him properly but the other folks are nasty to him. That's why he entreats the Lord to intervene and rescue him, instead of getting angry with him. He is after all the victim and deserves every consideration.

Parāku nīk ēlarā
Raga *Kiraṇāvaḷi*

p. parāku nīk ēlarā rāma

a. carācaramula vasiyincē ō
sārasākṣa nā panul anṭē yī

c. purāna śabari yosanginayaṭu nē
bhujincukonna śēṣamā rāma
dharā talamuna guhuni vale patra
talpam onarcitinā śrī tyāgarājupai

Why are you indifferent
to my needs, O Rama the Omnipresent?

Did I offer you left-over fruit like Śabari,
or make you sleep on a bed of leaves like
Guha?

Gloss
Since Tyagaraja didn't do either, the Lord should take care of him forthwith. No further need to delay granting his request. Since He is present everywhere and in all things moving and unmoving, there is no way He can ignore his devotee. Unless, of course, he "offended" Him by offering Him partly consumed food or made Him sleep on the ground. The impact of the song derives from the fact that the two people cited in the song are among the greatest of His devotees! So the lyricist employs irony to stress his eligibility for His grace.

Pāhi ramā ramaṇa
Raga *Varāḷi*

p. pāhi ramā ramaṇa mām pāhi sadguṇa gaṇa harē rāma

c1. cinta māna nīdu karuṇa isumanta rādu harē rāma

c2. entani sairintu nēnēmani vēgintu harē rāma

c3. ahaha ciluka kūna brahmāstramunaku tagunā harē rāma

c4. cēti malle puvvu guṇḍrātikōrvapōdu harē rāma

c5. dōsa paṇḍukeṭṭu rāma tōcuninupa kaṭṭu harē rāma

c6. deva deva venna kattidebbakōrcukonunā harē rāma

c7. talli taṇḍri brōvakuṇṭē tanayunikē drōva harē rāma

c8. rāja varya saraṇa tyāgarāja vinuta caraṇa harē rāma

Rama, be kind to me!
Though I constantly think of you,
I do not see any signs of your mercy,
I am at the end of my tether,
unable to endure the suffering,
I am being disproportionately punished.

Would you use a shotgun to bag a baby parrot,
grind a tender jasmine against a rock,
crunch a ripe cucumber against the iron fencing,
or slice a stick of butter with a sword?

If parents abandon the child,
who will come to its rescue?

Gloss

Tyagaraja often complains that he is being unfairly treated by the Lord and is being punished for minor shortcomings. In this, he is being a typical devotee, who thinks he deserves better. Minor sound effects stress the poignance of the message.

Parāmukham ēlarā rāmayya
Raga *Surați*

p. parāmukham ēlarā rāmayya

a. nirādaraṇa kaladā nī yeḍa
nityānanda kalyāṇa guṇa

c. ibha rāju nīk ēmainan iccenā telupu
śubha praduḍu nīvē yanucu
sundara tyāgarāja nuta

Why do you turn the other way, Rama,

have I slighted you ever?

Tell me, did the king of pachyderms
give you an incentive
saying you were propitious?

Gloss

Tyagaraja often brings up the fact that he is impecunious and cannot offer the Lord anything in return for His kindness. He also questions the Lord whether He helps only the wealthy, and whether He helps the poor at all. Obviously, he is being sarcastic, while trying to make the point that the Lord has been disregarding his pleas for redemption. This is one of the modalities of devotion.

Paṭṭi viḍuva rādu
Raga *Manjari*

p. paṭṭi viḍuva rādu nā ceyi
paṭṭi viḍuva rādu

a. puṭṭina nāḍē nija bhaktini meḍa
kaṭṭi guṭṭu cedaraka brōci ceyi

p. nity ānityamulanu bōdhinci
kṛty ākṛtyamulanu telipinci
pratyēkuḍu nīv ani kanipinci
bhṛtyuḍ aina tyāgarāju ceyi

Don't let go of my hand, Rama,

please don't let go of it.

You gifted me bhakti for you
the day I was born
and have ensured that I
cherish it steadfastly since.

You taught me the difference
between the lasting and the fleeting,
and the proper and the improper,
proving that you are the One
for this follower of yours.

Gloss

Tyagaraja gratefully recollects that the Lord first held his hand when he was born and has continued his support throughout his life teaching him about the Real and the Unreal, and appropriate and inappropriate action. This is a unique relationship that the saint has always enjoyed with the Lord. Double *-t-* in the first four lines and *-ty-* in the next four supply the requisite sound effects to the lyric. Note that Tyagaraja does not casually throw his sounds around: they are perfectly matched to the purport of each lyric and their intended effect on the audience when performed.

Prārabdham iṭṭunḍagan orulanu
Raga *Svarāvali*

p. prārabdham iṭṭ unḍagan orula nana
pani lēdu nīv unḍaga

a. bāla guṇa śīla jana pāla varada
kṛp ālavāla kāl ātīta śūla dhara vinuta nā

c. upakāri nēn aitē apakārul ayyedaru
kṛpa jūcitē migula nepamul encedarayya
capala cittulu bhakta vēṣulai nanu jūci
śatruvul ayyedaru śrī tyāgarāj āpta nā

Why blame others
when it is my fate,
with you looking after me?

I help others, they hate me,
I am kind to them, they fault me,
phony folks parading as paragons,
turn into my foes.

Gloss
This is self-pity on the part of the devotee that, in spite of the Lord looking after him, he has bad luck with fraudsters who pose as pious people and blame him for everything. They try to depict his good deeds as evil actions deliberately.

This is Tyagaraja's running criticism of the wicked elements in the society. His solution is that we ignore them and get on with our devotional pursuits and let the Lord deal with them, because there will never be a society without its ugly element. There was never a time in history when in some part of the globe there wasn't an upheaval, including in Tyagaraja's own milieu.

Rāma nīpai tanaku
Raga *Kēdāram*

p. rāma nīpai tanaku prēma pōdu sītā (rāma)

a. tāmarasa nayana nīdēmō māya kāni (rāma)

c1. manasu nī padamulanē jēra
kanulu nī rūpamunē kōra
vinu nī pērulakē nōrūra
tanapai idi nī karuṇērā (rāma)

c2. jananījanakāptulanyulu
dhana kanaka guru vēlpulu
dinamu nīvēyani māṭalu
anagha ivi nā bhūṣaṇamulu (rāma)

c3. bhōgānubhavamulandu
bāguga buddhi nīyandu
tyāgarājuni hṛdayamandu
vāgīśānandamandu (rāma)

My adoration for you never ceases, Rama—

My mind ever hovers around your feet
my eyes yearn to see your form
I drool over your name—
all due to your grace.

I treasure the words
that you are the mother, father,
kinsman, wealth, and mentor of all.

Amidst worldly pleasures,
you alone I see
and experience Supreme Bliss.

Gloss
This is the state of mind of the perfect devotee who worships the Lord. He sees, hears, and utters nothing but the name of the

Lord. Tyagaraja elsewhere also tells us about the benefits that devotees derive from a single-minded devotion to Rama. This is a 'textbook example' of mature bhakti.

Rāma rāma rāma nāpai
Raga *Kalyāṇi*

p. rāma rāma rāma nāpai nī daya
rāka yuṇḍa vaccunā ō rāma

c1. tanayuni ē jātiyaina brōvani
talliyu bhuvini kaladā ō rāma (rāma)

c2. tanaku tānu vañcana cēsukonu
dhanavantuḍu kalaḍā ō rāma (rāma)

c3. ilanu niścayamuga nīvu lēni
tāvendainanu kaladā ō rāma (rāma)

c4. sutuni māṭaku tallidaṇḍrulu
asūya paḍuṭa kaladā ō rāma (rāma)

c5. brahma niṣṭhuḍainaṭṭi yā ghanuniki
prabala vañcana kaladā ō rāma (rāma)

c6. tolli jēyu karmamanubhavimpakanu
tōyu vāru kalarā ō rāma (rāma)

c7. kanaka taruṇul āsa lēni saṁsārulu
kalalainanu kalarā ō rāma (rāma)

c8. nirvikāra śrī tyāgarājuniki
ninnu vinā kalarā ō rāma (rāma)

I have no doubt that you love me, Rama.

There's no mother on earth
who does not care for her son,
no affluent person that cheats himself;
there's no corner of the world where you are not;

There are no parents who envy their own children,
And no sage who is fooled by others;

No one's exempt from the laws of karma,
no householder who does not covet
women and wealth.

You are everything to unattached Tyagaraja.

Gloss

In an apparent self-confirmation, Tyagaraja adduces a number of evidentiary items that prove that it is the Lord's nature to love His devotees. He just cannot help spreading His love and extending His grace to those who surrender to Him. This song guarantees that liberation is available to one and all if they are so inclined.

Rāma sīta rāma
Raga *Balahamsa*

p. rāma sīta rāma rāma rāja tanaya rāma daśaratha rāma
sītā rāma rāma raghu kulābdhi sōma

c1. uragamulu penaginaṭl unnadi nā manasu
karuṇa jēsi kanṭa jūci karamu paṭṭu rāma

c2. satsati pati sēva sēyu candamuna nā manasu
utsavamulu sēyuṭakuppongenu rāma

c3. kalpa bhūjamuna tīga kaṭṭu rīti manasu
kalpamul ennaina viḍaci kadaladu śrī rāma

c4. advaita sāmrājyamul abbinaṭṭu rāma
sadvairāgyamunidiyu sāyujyamē rāma

c5. āgama nigamamulakun arthamidi rāma
tyāgarājucē cēyinci bhōgamandu rāma

My mind feels like it's the battleground of snakes,
please pacify it by showing your mercy.

I am raring to worship you like Sita did,
my mind is forever entwined around you
like the vines around the Wish-fulfilling Tree—
This is the divine union
spoken of in the scriptures.

Gloss

The *pallavi* kind of makes you think that the devotee imagines himself hugging his Lord repeatedly. The repetition of the name Rama so many times in a single line kind of tells us that the devotee cannot and should not ignore the Lord. In subsequent lines, the closeness-to-the-Lord idea is reinforced until the 'punch line' that the devotee *knows* he is one with the Lord. Amazing how skilled writers can express potent sentiments simply by repeating a single selected word.

Rūkalu padi vēlunna
Raga *Deśīya Tōḍi*

p. rūkalu padi vēl unna cēreḍu
nūkalu gati kāni ō manasā

a. kōkalu veyy unna
kaṭṭukonuṭak okaṭi kāni ō manasā

c. ūr ēlina tā panḍuṭa mūḍu mūra tāvu kāni
nūru bhakṣaṇamul abbina entō nōṭik anta kāni
ēru ninḍuga pārina pātraku tagu nīru vaccu kāni
sārataruni harini tyāgarāja sannutuni maravakē
manasā

Millionaires can eat only
measured amounts of food;

Out of a bursting wardrobe,
you wear only a single garment;

The ruler of a vast country
sleeps only on a six-foot bed;

Out of a hundred dishes offered,
one eats only a mouthful.

You can get only your bucketful
from a flooded river.

Never forget
the Almighty Lord.

Gloss

The message here is that there is no point in acquiring worldly possessions and accumulating wealth, because all you need to survive is food on the table, roof over your head, and a robe over your body to protect you from the elements. Beyond that, whatever you possess is meaningless for your existence. You'd think this is obvious, but we need the philosopher to tell it to us. So, instead of getting caught in the rat race, one should meditate on the Lord whose grace is boundless, will flow toward you, and will redeem you from self-destruction. In reality, life is simple; we are good at making a mess of it.

Sākṣi lēdanucu sādhimpakē
Raga *Bangālā*

p. sākṣi lēd anucu sādhimpakē
satya sandha sad bhakta pālaka

a. vīkṣak ādul ella navvarā
sākṣi vamśa nīradhi pūrṇa candra

c. śakti nī yeḍa ninḍāra lēdā parā
śakti brōva lēdā viṣayam andu
virakti kalgu śrī tyāgarājuni nija
bhakti nīv eruga lēvā mānavula

Don't say there's no evidence,
Upholder of Truth and Refuge of true
devotees!

That'd be laughable,
O Scion of the Solar race.

You are omniscient—
did *parāśakti* not protect me before?
you know yourself
that I am averse to the world,
and that I am a true devotee.

Gloss
This is another way of pleading by the devotee that, whether or not someone knows about it, he is a true devotee of the Lord and that He should know it. He is omniscient. The assertion is that the Lord knows everything and a devotee's earnestness will not go unnoticed. Sincerity of devotion is what matters.

Samukhāna nilva kalgunā
Raga *Kōkila Varāḷi*

p. samukhāna nilva kalgunā kamalāsana

a. kṣama kalgu bhū tanaya lakṣmaṇ ādi
mahātmulakē kāni anyulaku

c. kamal āsanād yamara dik patulu
kalaśa vāridhilō jūḍa nēraka
gumi kūḍi moral iḍa kāryamulu
konasāgen aṭa tyāgarāja vinuta

It's not easy to meet with Rama,

if you are not Sita, Lakshmana,
or their equals in piety.

Brahma, Indra, and others

could not gain His audience.
so they appealed to Him as a group
and achieved their purpose.

Gloss

The idea is that the Lord is difficult of access to the common man, so a group of similar-minded people had to approach Him together to reach their goal. It's a way of praising the Lord, and stressing our own lowliness. Looks like Tyagaraja was thinking of every possible means of approaching the Lord to gain His audience.

Sandēhamunu tīrpum ayya
Raga *Rāmapriya*

p. sandēhamunu tīrpum ayya
sākēta nilaya rāmayya

a. nand ārcita pada yugamulu mēlo
nāgarīkam agu pādukā yugambulu mēlo

c. vara maunul ella caraṇambulanu
smariyimpa nīdu padam osangenē
bharat ārcanacē pādukalu
dhara ninn osangē tyāgarāju bhāgyamā

I have a question for you,
Rama of Saketa—

which are better:
your feet worshipped by the gods,
or your sandals

reverently carried by Bharata
that reminded the sages
of your presence?

Gloss

This is a clever way of praising Rama as someone whose feet are venerated as the refuge of devotees. It is good to actually bow to His feet but, when it's not possible, the sandals that once adorned His feet, will have to do. In the mind of His brother Bharata, they represent the wearer Himself. The sages feel His presence when they look at them. Thus, in the minds of everyone the Sandals are the Lord Himself. We use the phrase in English, "no one can fill his shoes" to describe the greatness of the original wearer, who is hard to replace. Thus, shoes are symbolic of the person that wears them. In this case, then, there is no difference between the footwear and the wearer in the minds of the devotees. Humans are fond of symbols; they tend to be real in their minds. A worshipped idol is never a piece of stone to them, *and* it works for them.

Sarasa sāma dāna
Raga *Kāpi Nārāyaṇi*

p. sarasa sāma dāna bhēda danḍa catura
sāṭi daivam evarē brōvavē

a. parama śāmbhav āgrēsarunḍ agucu
palku rāvaṇuḍu teliyalēka pōye

c. hitavu māṭal entō bāga palkitivi
satamugān ayōdhyan ittun anṭivi
nata sahōdaruni rāju cēsi rāka
hatamu jēsitivi tyāgarāja nuta

Show me your grace, Lord,
you are adept in the four kinds
of statecraft. No god equals you.
The great Siva devotee, Ravana,
did not comprehend
your words of conciliation
and declined the offer of Ayodhya;
you slew him before making
his brother king of Lanka.

Gloss

Apparently, there are some discrepancies in the events narrated here compared to Valmiki's rendition of them, but that's beside the point. One who fails to understand the Lord's intentions and ignores His advice comes to grief. In the infinitude of His love, He means well by one and all. This *kṛti* achieved mid-level popularity from time to time.

Vanaja nayanuḍ ani
Raga *Kēdāragauḷa*

p. vanaja nayanuḍ ani valacitivō vāni
manasuna daya lēdē

a. munupaṭi caritamulanu viniyunna
vanita svabhāvamu valana śrī rāmuni

c. orula bādhalaku ōrvaka yunḍuṭa
parama dharmam anucu bāguga palkunu
varaduḍu āśrita vatsaluḍ ani pērē
dhara jayam osangu śrī tyāgarāja vinutuni

Did you fall in love with His charming eyes?
He's heartless, though.

You may have loved Him just like a woman
who has heard her lover's past exploits,
but He's without compassion.

He's reputed to save those who surrender to Him,
and teach people not to ignore those who suffer,
but He has no pity Himself.

Gloss

Tyagaraja is probably addressing his mind in this song in which he tells it that the Lord is totally merciless, even though he preaches that it is not nice to ignore those who are suffering. The lyric is an example of praise through reproach. On the one hand, the devotee acknowledges the exploits and the charm of Rama and, on the other hand, claims He has no compassion for anyone. The first four lines have the recurring *n* sound and the last four have the familiar *r*.

Vinatā suta vāhana

Raga *Jayantasēna*

p. vinatā suta vāhana śrī ramaṇa
manas āraga sēvinceda rāma

a. ninu sāreku jūḍani bratuk ēla
manujulan ēceḍu jīvanam ēla

c. mata bhēdam anē segan ārcaga
sammata vākkulu palkuṭa sukhamā
kṣitilō sat sangati saukhyamu

pālita tyāgarāj āmara pūjita

O Garuda-riding Lord,
I worship you whole-heartedly.

Life without seeing you joyously
is useless. Life tormenting others
is a total waste.

Without reconciling the sects,
pacifying words are fruitless.
Good people are the best company.

Gloss
As in every other social milieu, Tyagaraja experienced his share of religious differences and sectarian struggles, in addition to whatever social evils and political turmoil existed during his time. He effectively isolated himself in his spiritual life and music, thereby living at peace with the world. So he is quite qualified to talk about such things. Nothing unique about the lyric in terms of literary devices. There is a modest presence of *n* in the first half.

Yocanā kamala lōcanā
Raga *Darbār*

p. yōcanā kamala lōcanā nanu brōva

a. sūcana teliyakan orula
yācana sētun anucu nīku
tōcenā dyuti vijit āyuta
virōcana nannu brovan ika

c. kēcana nija bhakta nicaya pāpa
vimōcana kala birudul ella koni
nann ēcanā kṛta vipina cara
var ābhiṣēcana tyāgarāja pūjita

Are you debating whether to redeem me?

You think I will approach other gods,
not having an inkling of your mind?

Did you pick up all those titles
of saving devotees just to tease me,
O Lotus-eyed Rama?

Gloss

Tyagaraja here is getting personal with the Lord and demands to know what He is thinking in regard to providing refuge to him. In case the Lord has any questions about His devotee's *bona fides,* he rhetorically convinces Him that he has every indication that he will be saved for sure.

SECTION III

MEDITATIONS

In quite a few songs, Tyagaraja just offers simple prayers to the Lord, without any circumlocution or indirection. They sometimes take the form of descriptions of the Lord's appearance on different occasions that appeal to the devotee and help focus his attention. The devotee tries to identify himself with the Lord in all aspects of His deportment. He enjoys the simple bliss of being in His presence. That kind of a quiescent self-absorbed mood is called meditation here. When all is said and done, one simply *is* and remains one's own *Self.*

Anāthuḍanu kānu rāma
Raga *Jinglā*

p. anāthuḍanu kānu rāma nē(n)

a. anāthuḍavu nīv ani nigamajñula
sanātanula māṭa vinnānu nē(n)

c. nirādaruvu jūci yī kali
narādhamul anedaru
purāṇa puruṣa pura ripu nuta
nāga rāṭ śayana tyāgarāja nuta nē(n)

I am not forlorn—
you are.

There's none to protect you,
but I have you!

Seeing me neglected by you,
worthless people say
that I am helpless.

But I heard the sages say
that you are the savior
of saviors, O Ancient One!

Gloss

This is a play on the word *anātha,* which can mean either one who is abandoned, or one who is the head honcho, the top person, in this case the Lord Himself. The bard is particularly fond of this type of word-play.

Anupama guṇāmbudhi
Raga *Aṭhāṇā*

p. anupama guṇāmbudhi yani ninnu nera nammi-
yanusarincina vāḍanaiti

a. manupakayē yunnāvu manu patī vrāsi
mēm anupa māk evaru vinumā daya rāni

c1. janaka jāmātavai janakajā mātavai
janaka jālamu cālu cālunu hari

c2. kanaka paṭa dhara nannu kana kapaṭam ēla tanu
kanaka paṭhanamu sētu kāni pūni

c3. kala lōna nīvē sakala lōka nātha
kōkalu lōkuva kanicci kāchinadi vini

c4. rāja kula kalaśābdhi rāja sura pāla gaja
rāja rakṣaka tyāgarāja vinuta

Trusting you as the wellspring of virtue
I followed you.

But you ignore me.
Through whom can I send word,
O Merciless One!

Son-in-law of Janaka, patient like the Earth
(the Mother of Sita)
O Father, tarry no more, O Hari!

O Golden-garmented one!

Why stall for time though I keep repeating
your name,

dreaming about you,
hearing how you saved the modesty of helpless
(Draupadi)?

Gloss
A direct prayer to Rama, the beauty of this lyric derives from the composer's splitting of repetitive words, based on his proficiency in Sanskrit, e.g. *Janaka jāmāta* (son-in-law)/ *Jankakajā* (Sita) *mātā;* and *kanaka paṭa* (gold garment)/*kana kapaṭa* (delay in helping); with further repetitions for added emphasis.

Bhajana sēya rādā
Raga *Aṭhāṇā*

p. bhajana sēya rādā rāma

a. aja rudr ādulaku satatam ātma mantram aina rāma

c1. karagu bangāru valva kaṭin entō merayaga
ciru navvulu gala mukhamunu cintinci cintinci

c2. aruṇ ābh ādharamunu surucira dant āvaḷini
merayu kapōla yugamunu niratamunanu talaci talaci

c3. bāguga mānasa bhava sāgaramunanu tarimpa
tyāgarāju manavini vini tārakamagu rāma nāma

Worship Rama whose name is a mantra

close to the hearts of Brahma and Śiva —

Seeing the glint of His gilded garments
around His waist, and looking into His smiling face,
His lips shimmering bright, and lovely teeth
set inside the cheeks, meditate
to cross the ocean of samsara.

Gloss

Every once in a while, Tyagaraja reminds us of the physical attributes of Rama and exhorts us to meditate on them so we will not backslide into our material selves. No further prodding is necessary to keep us on our toes.

Bhajana sēyu mārgamunu

Raga *Nārāyaṇi*

p. bhajana sēyu mārgamunu jūpavē parama
bhāgavata bhāgadhēya sad

a. ajuḍu rudr ākhaṇḍala pavanaja
vijay ādulu gumi gūḍi nīdu caraṇa

c. sakala vēda śāstra purāṇādi dīpa
sakala mantra tantra rūpa
sakala dēva ripu samara pratāpa
sādhu tyāgarāja nuta śrī rāma nija

Teach us how to worship you properly,
O Rama, the be-all and end-all of existence.

Tell us how Brahma, Indra, Hanuman
and Vijaya (Arjuna) served you.
You are all the sciences and the Vedas
in Person.

Gloss

Before you pray to Rama, you have to know how to offer your prayers to Him. Fortunately, He has been worshipped by many illustrious personages, so we can follow their example. Or, easier still, we can ask Rama Himself to help us out—which is what Tyagaraja does here. He does that in a lyric in which there are three sets of words that generate the sound effects: (1) alliterative, initial consonant repeated: *bhajana, bhāgavata, bhāgadhēya;* (2) Second or later sound in the word repeated: *ajuḍu, pavanaja, vijaya;* and (3) rhymes: *dīpa, rūpa, sītāpa, pratāpa.* Repetitive sounds modulate not only the tempo of the song but also enhance audience response. Who knows, even Rama may be impressed and be inclined to grant the devotee's supplications.

Ennaḍu jūtunō
Raga *Kaḷāvati*

p. ennaḍu jūtunō ina kula tilaka ninn (ennaḍu)

a. pannaga śayana bhakta janāvana
punnama canduru pōlu mukhamunu

c. dharaṇijā saumitri bharata ripughna
vānara yūdha pati varuḍānjanēyuḍu
karuṇanu okarik okaru varṇimpa-
nādaraṇanu pilicē ninnu tyāgarāj ārcita

O Gem among the Solar rulers,

When will I see the moon-like face
of the refuge of worshipers,
resting on the serpent-bed,
as Sita, Lakshmana, Bharata,
Śatrughna and the mighty Hanuman
praise you, and affectionately address you?

Gloss
Tyagaraja's apparent impatience is a mark of his legendary patience when it comes to his longing to get a glimpse of the Lord. Here he asks Him why He is ignoring him, even as He individually pays attention to His companions. He is right there worshipping Him, as well!

Not many sound effects except the double-*n* in the first words of the first three lines.

Enta pāpinaiti
Raga *Gauḷipantu*

p. enta pāpin aitin ēmi sēyudu hā
ēlāgu tāḷudunē ō rāma

a. anta duḥkhamulanu tīrcu harini jūci
enta vār ainanu bāya sahinturē

c1. maccikatō tānu muccaṭāḍi mōsa
bucci yēca madi vaccenō kaṭa kaṭā

c2. āsa minci āyāsa paḍanu vidhi
vrāsunā nā muddu vēsuni kānamē

c3. sēva jēyuṭē jīvanam aniyunṭi
daivamā nā pāli bhāgyam iṭlāyanē

c4. rājillu srī tyāgarāju tā pongucu
pūjincu śrī raghu rāj indu lēnandu(kenta)

I have sinned so much
I cannot cope with it myself.

Having seen Hari, the destroyer of misery,
can anyone let go of Him?

How could He abandon me thus,
having sweetly conversed with me?

I won't be greedy, but
is it destined that I see Him?

Having dedicated my life to His service,
it's my fate to pine for Him thus!

Gloss

The lyricist laments his inability to see the Lord again and again. It just does not happen despite his insatiable desire to do so and his incessant effort. The tone is one of desperation, hopelessness, and resignation—all of which, of course, are part of the devotee's progression toward his goal.

Enta rāni
Raga *Hari Kāmbhoji*

p. enta rāni tanak enta pōni nī centa viḍuva jāla śrī rāma

a. antakāri nī centa jēri hanumantuḍai koluva lēdā

c1. śēṣuḍu śivuniki bhūṣuḍu lakṣmaṇa vēṣiyai koluva lēdā

c2. śiṣṭuḍu mauni variṣṭhuḍu goppa vaśiṣṭhuḍu hituḍu gālēdā

c3. nara vara nīkai sura gaṇamulu vānarulai koluvaga lēdā

c4. āgamōktamagu nī guṇamulu śrī tyāgarāju pogaḍaga lēdā

Come what may,
I am not leaving you—

Śiva served you as Hanuman;
Śesha the serpent transformed
into Lakshmana to be with you;
the pre-eminent Vaśishtha
became your family counselor;
the gods in heaven yearned
to help you as monkey hosts.

Tyagaraja sings your praises
indexed in the Scripture.

Gloss

As appropriate to the melody *Hari Kāmbhoji,* Tyagaraja liberally employs two- and three-syllable and longer rhyming words in each of the couplets in the song. The *pallavi* and *anupallavi* use the same *-nta* rhyme to set the tone and rhythm of the lyric. Also, note that the lyric starts with two-syllable rhymes, then the rhyming extends to three- and four-syllables, before a series of short two-syllable words round out the cadence of the lyric. The composer has an infinite variety of tricks up his sleeve. The cumulative effect of the alternating rhyming patterns must be stunning when the song is performed. Tyagaraja is making sure that the impact of his lyric directly reaches the Lord's ears!

Enta vēḍukondu
Raga *Sarasvatī Manohari*

p. enta vēḍukondu rāghava
pantam ēlarā ō rāghava

a. cinta tīrcutak enta mōḍirā
antarātma nā centa rānu nē(n)

c. cittam andu ninnu jūcu saukhyamē
uttamamb anucun uppongucunu
satta mātramā cāla nammitini
sārvabhauma śrī tyāgarāja nuta

How long should I beg you,
why are you so adamant, Raghava?

Why do you balk to relieve my misery
and help me realize myself?

I believed earnestly
that seeing you within my heart
is the best existence.

Gloss

This is a straightforward supplication to the Lord to show Himself soon. But even in such a short song, Tyagaraja doesn't forget his forceful deployment of effective, rhyming words. The first four lines use the familiar *-nta* rhymes and three of the next four have words with *-tta*. Part of songwriting always involves sound effects based on the placement of words; in the case of Tyagaraja, it is a lot more than just a musical device. It is an outpouring of his heart linked to his yearning to merge with his Lord.

Eṭlā dorikitivō
Raga *Vasanta*

p. eṭlā dorikitivō rāma tana(k)

a. cuṭlāra gaḍiya dōvaku nādu
paṭl ābhimānamu lēkunḍaga

c. pāda mahimō pedda-
lāśīrvāda balamō susvarapu
nāda phalamō tyāgarāja
khēda hara śrīnātha tana(k)

I am amazed that
I ever knew about you,

for no one around me
ever shows me consideration.

It must be my surrender at your feet
or the good wishes of the elders
or the power of my perfect musical notes.

Gloss

On a somewhat happier note, the usually complaining devotee expresses satisfaction that he has found the Lord, owing to his great good fortune, or he is blessed by virtuous elders, or due to the innate power of the sounds of his powerful music. Note the use of the term *nāda,* which the composer visits over and over again and attributes divine powers to it. The first three lines repeat the *-ṭl-* combination, while the last four use the dissyllabic *-āda* rhyme. We can speculate that the first set suggests effort by the combination of the harsh *ṭ* with the lateral *l,* while the second set uses the single voiced consonant *d,* which is easier on the ears. Did Tyagaraja do all this consciously in each of his songs? Why not? He wanted to create just the right effect through each one of his compositions. To him, the *geya* was an instrument of spiritual emancipation, no less.

Evar unnāru brōva
Raga *Māḷava Śrī*

p. evarunnāru brōva
inta tāmasam ēla nayya

a. vivarambuga telupavayya
viśveśa śrī pañca nadīśa

c. manas āraga dhyānimpanu
manasu nilupu marmambu telisi
tana vāḍanē talaci dhairyam-
osagu tyāgarāja vinuta

Who will save me, Śiva, and
why this tardiness in doing so?
Pray tell
so I can restrain my mind
and focus it. Give me strength,
considering me your own.

Gloss
The strength needed to meditate on the Lord must also come from the Lord. Hence the basis of morality is the Lord Himself. There is an apparent circularity in the argument that you need to be morally upright to become a true devotee, and only a true devotee can live an unblemished life. In other words, morality and devotion are co-extensive, and one cannot have the one without the other. Intriguing, isn't it?

Gītārthamu sangītānandamunu
Raga *Suraṭi*

p. gītārthamu sangīt ānandamun
ī tāvuna jūḍarā ō manasā

a. sītā pati caraṇ ābjamul iḍukonna
vāt ātmajuniki bāga telusurā

c. hari hara bhāskara kāl ādi
karmamulanu matamula marmamulan eringina

hari vara rūpuḍu harihaya vinutuḍu
vara tyāgarāja varaduḍu sukhirā

Look here for heavenly music
and the divine message of the Gita.

Hanuman learned it
at the feet of Rama,
as he mastered the secrets
of all the sects.

Gloss
The implication here again is that music is the best vehicle of acquiring spiritual knowledge when conveyed through appropriate words in song. The Gita makes one a devotee, and the combination of knowledge and song will lead to liberation, as the saint mentions in other songs as well.

Ennāḷḷu tirigēdi
Raga *Māḷava Śrī*

p. ennāḷḷu tirigēdi yennāḷḷu

a. enna rāni dēhamul etti yī samsāra gahanam andu
pannuga cōrula rīti parulanu vēgincucunu

c1. rēpaṭi kūṭiki lēd ani rēyi pagalu vesanam ondi
śrī pati pūjala maraci cēsinaṭṭi vāri vale

c2. uppu karupūramu varakun unchavṛtti cēn ārjinci
meppulaku poṭṭa nimpi mēmē peddalam anucu

c3. bhramanu koni irugu porugu bhakṣimpa rammani pilva
amarucukō pūja japamu nā sāyamu cētun anucu

c4. nā yanduṇḍe tappulu nāḍe telusukonṭini kāni
bāya viḍuvaka mahānubhāva tyāgarāja vinuta

How many times have I been reborn
and wandered in this dense forest
tormenting others like a robber,

worrying about the next day's meal
ignoring the worship of the Lord,

earning a living through alms
while faking respectability,

and promising help with worship
when neighbors invite me for food?

I am aware of my shortcomings,
yet I cannot get rid of them.

Gloss
This is a confessional kind of lyric, which often appears in Tyagaraja's *kṛti* corpus. Of course, there can never be enough repentance for a devotee, that is, until his goal of seeing his Lord has been attained. The uniqueness of this composition lies in its utter honesty and the reiteration of the fact that, while knowing one's faults is a good first step, in practice, getting rid of those faults is quite another matter.

Ēm ani pogaḍudurā
Raga *Vīra Vasanta*

p. ēm ani pogaḍudurā śrī rāma

a. śrīman nabhō maṇi vamśa lalāma
bhuvana vāsi mā rāma ninn (ēmani)

c. śivuniki tāmasa guṇam icci kamala
bhavuniki rājasa guṇa mosagi śacī
dhavuni garva hṛdayunigā jēsina
dāśarathī tyāgarāja vinuta ninn (ēmani)

O Rama, I cannot praise you enough—

You bestowed tāmasa on Śiva,
and rājasa on Brahma, making Indra
hotheaded.

Gloss

Tyagaraja makes it appear that, Rama (Vishnu) being a master strategist, He saved the best attribute *sattva* for Himself, so that He could maintain harmony in the universe. Indra was all puffed up because he was the head honcho of heavenly bodies, a role that was appropriate for him. Brahma passionately created everything, and Siva ended everything. But Rama's role as the preserver of the universe is the most admirable and auspicious, and hence praiseworthy.

Ēṭi yocanalu jēsēvu
Raga *Kiraṇāvaḷi*

p. ēṭi yōcanalu jēsēvurā
eduru palku vār evaru lērurā

a. nōṭi māṭa jārcaga rādurā
kōṭi vēlpulalō mēti yaina nī

c. meṇḍu śūrulalō venuka tīyav ani
reṇḍu māṭal āḍe vāḍu kādani
aṇḍa kōṭla pālincu vāḍ ani
caṇḍa maunul āḍa tyāgarāja nuta

What are you thinking?
No one is going to cross you.

You cannot go back on your word,
mightiest of the mighty.

The sages declare
that you are a man of your word
and you rule the universe.

Gloss
In an interesting twist of the normal situation, in this song, the devotee advises the Lord to think straight and protect His reputation as a man of His word. The Lord cannot afford to tarnish his fame by failing to keep his promise of rescuing the forlorn. Note the *-nd-* rhymes in the last verse.

Kamal āpta kula
Raga *Bṛndāvana Sāranga*

p. kamal āpta kula kalaśābdhi candra
kāvavayya nannu karuṇā samudra

a. kamalā kaḷatra kausalyā suputra
kamanīya gātra kāmāri mitra

c. munu dāsula brōcinad ella cāla
vini nī caraṇ āśrituḍ aitinayya
kanikarambuna nāk abhayam ivvumayya
vanaja lōcana śrī tyāgarāja nuta

Scion of the Solar Race,
take good care of me, kind Lord,

Having heard that you helped out
all your devotees, I fell at your feet;
show mercy, and reassure me.

Gloss
In this song and many others, Tyagaraja claims that he deserves the Lord's protection based on the fact that He had previously saved all his devotees. The implication is that He has no choice now but to save him, too.

Kanugonṭini śrī rāmuni nēdu
Raga *Bilahari*

p. kanugonṭini śrī rāmuni nēḍu

a. ina kulam andu impu gānu puṭṭina
ila lōna śītā nāyakuni nēḍu

c. bharata lakṣmaṇa śatrughnulu koluva
pavamāna sutuḍu pādamula paṭṭa
dhīrul aina sugrīva pramukhulu
vinuti sēya tyāgarāja nutuni nēḍu

I have seen Sri Rama today—

Born in the Solar House,
attended by Bharata, Lakshmana,
and Satrughna,
Hanuman at His feet, and
warriors like Sugriva
singing his glory.

Gloss
Tyagaraja has these frequent visions of Rama waited on by his retinue, which would indicate that he is constantly immersed in the world of Rama. His graphic lyrics depicting Rama's entourage contain a great variety of minute detail, which bring the scenes before our minds even as he experiences them.

Lakṣaṇamulu gala
Raga *Śuddha Sāvēri*

p. lakṣaṇamulu gala rāmuniki
pradakṣiṇam onarintumu rārē

a. kukṣini brahmāṇḍambul unnav aṭa
vicakṣaṇuḍ aṭa dīkṣā guruḍ aṭa śubha

c. lakṣaṇa lakṣyamu gala śrutulaku pratyakṣamb aunaṭa
śikṣa paḍi sabhanu meppincu bhakta rakṣakuṇḍ aunaṭa
akṣarasthul aina bhajana parulakē antaranguḍ aunaṭa
sākṣiyai velayu tyāgarāja pakṣakuḍ aunata muppadi reṇḍu

Let's walk around Sri Rama and honor
Him who manifests the most blessed traits—

He rules the universe justly,
and is the Supreme Preceptor;

He can be known through
the self-evident Vedas,
He is the mainstay of learned devotees,
and the best friend
of self-realized souls.
He is the Witness of all,
endowed with the thirty-two
felicitous bodily signs.

Gloss

Tyagaraja is never tired of describing the physical features of Rama, to which his fascination is riveted. But this is not just an inventory of His features: an entire philosophy is embedded in the song, proclaiming that the Lord is known by the Vedas, is a confidant of those who realize His true nature through self-discipline, and is the Witness of all that happens in the universe. While circumambulating such a Lord, we are promising to honor those features that make us great devotees. The cluster *-kṣa-* is obviously the dominant sound, intended to highlight the sense before our minds. It occurs in *every* line of the lyric, sometimes twice per line.

Lāvaṇya rāma kanulāra
Raga *Pūrṇa Ṣaḍjam/Rudrapriya*

p. lāvaṇya rāma kanulāra jūḍavē ati

a. śrī vanitā citta kumuda
śīta kara śat ānanyaja

c. nī manasu nī sogasu nī dinusu vērē
tāmasa mata daivam ēla tyāgarāja nuta divya

O handsome Rama,
won't you look kindly on me?
You are the moon that makes
the lotus of Lakshmi's mind bloom.

Your heart, your mind, and
your charm are superior
I don't want lesser gods
of unenlightened faiths.

Gloss

In this short lyric, Tyagaraja is happy to serve the charming Lord who is different than all the gods of ignorant faiths. It is thus a reinforcement of devotion to Rama and Rama alone, though the world offers many choices of deities to worship. His mind never wavers from its singular goal. No special effects have been attempted in the lyric, except the repeated consonants in *manasu, dinusu,* and *sogasu.* Give Tyagaraja a line, any line, and he sneaks in some sound effect. He won't let you forget it—ever!

Marakata maṇi varṇa
Raga *Varāḷi*

p. marakata maṇi varṇa rāma nannu
maravaka nā yanna

a. parama puruṣa binna brōvumu
dēvara śaraṇ anukonna

c. vara bhakta suparṇa vāhana
karuṇā rasa pūrṇa
dharaṇi tanayak unna prēma rasamu
tyāgarājuk ī yanna

O Emerald-complexioned Rama,
don't forget me.

Exalted Lord, lend me a helping hand
soon, you are my refuge.

O Garuda-riding Lord
brimming with compassion,
treat me as tenderly
as you do Sita.

Gloss

Double *nn* is the predominant sound here, which is used all through the *kṛti*. Tyagaraja boldly asks Rama to treat him as affectionately as He does His consort Sita. While in the case of ordinary people this might be considered arrogance, a true devotee has the right to claim his Lord as his own. In fact, ultimately, he doesn't view himself and the Lord as two separate entities, because the devotee obliterates his individual identity as his devotion climaxes.

Māṭāḍavēmi nātō
Raga *Nīlāmbari*

p. māṭ āḍavēmi nātō mādhurya pūrṇ ādhara

a. sāṭi dorakani rāma svāmi madi ranjilla

c. edur eduru jūci yendu kānaka nā
hṛdayamunak entō hitavu lēka
sadayuḍa nēn unḍaga samukhamu dorikitē
nīrada varṇa śrī tyāgarāj ārcita mudduga

Why aren't you talking with me,
you sweet-lipped Lord
who knows no equals,
to delight my heart?

Looking all over frustrated,
and finally finding you,
I am here in front of you—
Be kind, blue-tinged Lord.

Gloss
The devotee longs to chat with the Lord face to face, because nothing else satisfies him. This theme is repeated many times throughout the saint's lyrics, understandably. In *Śivānandalaharī* (24) Sankara wonders when he will be able to pass millions of years blissfully in the company of the auspicious god Śiva, praying to be redeemed by Him with his hands raised above his head.

Mēlukō dayānidhī
Raga *Saurāṣtra*

p. mēlukō dayānidhī mēlukō dāśarathī

a. mēlukō dayānidhī mitr ōdayamau vēḷa

c1. venna pālu bangāru ginnelo nēn uncinānu
tinnag āraginci tēṭa kannulatō nannu jūḍa

c2. nārad ādi munulu surulu vārija bhavuḍ indu
kaḷādharuḍu nī sannidhilō kōri koluvu kācināru

c3. rāja rāj ādi dig rājul ella vaccināru
rāja nīti teliya tyāgarāja vinuta nannu brōva

Wake up, my Lord,
the sun is rising.

Partake of the milk and butter
that I have ready for you
and cast your shining eyes on me.

Sages Narada and others,
and Brahma and Śiva await
an audience with you.

Gloss

It is customary in our temples and households to start the morning worship of the Lord with a supplication to Him to wake up and prepare for the daily rituals. Tyagaraja takes it one step further by also offering Him His favorite milk and butter for breakfast, while the sages, the gods, and rulers of the quarters wait to pay homage. Here and in several other lyrics, the composer makes sure that the Lord is well-groomed and well-fed and is in a happy mood, ready to bless His devotees.

Mērusamāna dhīra
Raga *Māyāmāḷavagauḷa*

p. mēru samāna dhīra varada raghu
vīra jūtāmu rārā mahā

a. sāra sāra oyyārapu naḍalanu
nīrada kāntini nī ṭhīvini mahā

c. alakala muddunu tilakapu tīrunu
taḷuku cekkulacē tanaru nemmōmunu
gaḷamuna śobhillu kanaka bhūṣaṇamula
daḷita durmānava tyāgarāj ārcita

Let me see your splendor,
your elegant gait, blue brilliance,
and your majesty,
O destroyer of evil people;

the beauty of your forelocks,
the dot between your brows,
shiny cheeks, lovely face,
and gold necklaces.

Gloss
Straightforward description of the Lord with His finery. The lyric is embellished with *r* rhymes in the first four lines and *l* rhymes in the last four lines. The first part uses long vowels in disyllabic words and the second short ones in trisyllabic words,

providing a contrasting movement. The short vowels indicate closure.

Mitri bhāgyamē
Raga *Kharaharapriya*

p. mitri bhāgyamē bhāgyamu manasā sau(mitri)

a. citra ratna maya śēṣa talpam andu
sītā patini unici yūcu sau(mitri)

c. bāguga vinta rāgamulan ālāpamu
sēyaga mēnu pulakarincaga
tyāgarāja nutuḍagu śrī rāmuni
tatv ārthamunu pogaḍi jūcu sau(mitri)

Saumitri is really lucky!

He places the Lord in
the jewel-bedecked serpent bed
and enjoys watching Him
as He swings back and forth;

in unique tunes does he
praise the true symbolism of the Lord
with his hairs standing on end.

Gloss
Tyagaraja enjoys describing the good fortune of the members of Rama's retinue, who serve Him in close proximity, something that is not available to the devotee. To all of them he applies spiritual music, which depends on the underlying

lyric. He doesn't sing in a vacuum or for its own sake. He sings specific songs in specific ragas to serve a specific purpose which, ultimately, lead to liberation.

Naḍaci naḍaci jūcēr ayōdhyā
Raga *Kharaharapriya*

p. naḍaci naḍaci jūcēr ayōdhyā
nagaramu kānarē

a. puḍami suta sahāyuḍai
pūrṇuni ātmārāmuni kūḍi yāḍa

c. aṭṭē kannulu kūrci teraci sūtramu
paṭṭi veliki vēṣa dhārulai
puṭṭu cāvu lēni tāvu teliyaka
pogaḍedaru tyāgarāja vinutuni

Trekking onerously all the way
to Ayodhya, they didn't find
Rama the Self, coupled with Sita.

Blinking their eyes meditatively,
spinning beads with their hands,
and attired impressively,
they never find their Source.

Gloss
A familiar theme of Tyagaraja's chastising poseurs who never find the Lord in their own hearts with all their ostentation. The double *t* rhymes in the verse clinch the issue once and for all forcefully. Also note that the saint stresses once again that the

devotee's goal is Self-Realization, with Rama as the symbol of the Self.

Nādōpasanacē
Raga *Bēgaḍa*

p. nādōpasanacē śankara nārāyaṇa vidhulu velasiri ō manasā

a. vēdōddhārulu vēdātītulu viśvamella niṇḍiyuṇḍē vāralu

c. mantrātmulu yantra tantrātmulu mari
manvantaramulennō kala vāralu
tantrī laya svara rāga vilōlulu
tyāgarāja vandyulu svatantrulu

The Trinity has evolved from nāda,
the mysterious universal hum:
the origin of the divinities in the universe,
and of those steeped in mantra and esoteric sciences,
and long-lived ones and musical prodigies.

Gloss
From the primal sound *nāda,* all existence is said to have evolved. It's even more esoteric than *mantra.* Music is just one example of it. It is also called a yoga in its own right. Tyagaraja, steeped in ancient wisdom, visited this topic from time to time across his lyrical output.

Nammi vaccina nannu
Raga *Kalyāṇi*

p. nammi vaccina nannu nayamuga brōvavē ninnu

a. kommani varamulan osagē kōvūri sundarēśa

c. vēda purāṇāgama śāstrādulu gumi gūḍi
pādamulu kana jālaka batimāli vēḍa
nāda rūpa śrī saundarya nāyakī patē bhēda
vāda rahita tyāgarāja varada sundarēśa ninu

Please take care of me,
I trust you, O Sundareśa,
who freely grants devotees' wishes.

All the scriptures together
Failed to learn your Source,
Consort of Saundarya Nāyakī,
and begged you, nāda personified.

You are beyond
all contrary depictions.

Gloss
Obviously written during or after his visit to Kovur at his friend's request, this song celebrates the Lord as Sundaresa. He is described here as the personification of *nāda,* the eternal hum that originates in one's heart and is the basis of all music. So, when Tyagaraja sings, he celebrates not just the external notes, but their spiritual source. The *caranam* employs the *d* rhyme: *vēda, pāda, nāda, vāda.*

Nārada gāna lōla

Raga *Aṭhāṇā*

p. nārada gāna lōla nata jana paripāla

a. nīrada sama nīla nirupama guṇa śīla

c. nīvu lēka yē tanuvulu niratamugā naḍucunu
nīvu lēka yē taruvulu nikkamugā molucunu
nīvu lēka yē vānalu nityamugā kuriyunu
nīvu lēka tyāgarāja nī guṇamulan eṭu pāḍunu

Lord, fond of Narada's melodies,
with the complexion of a cloud
and unmatched traits—

You animate all the forms,
you make the plants grow,
you make the rains fall;
But for you, Tyagaraja
has no one to sing about.

Gloss

This is one of the many lyrics by Tyagaraja where he praises the omnipotence of the Lord. The Lord is responsible for everything that happens in the world. The first two lines use the *l* rhyme in disyllabic words and repetition of the consonants *t, n,* and *b,* besides the initial phrase *nīvu lēka* in the four last lines. The repetition of the phrase four times clearly establishes that without the Lord, nothing so much as moves in the world.

Nata jana paripāla
Raga *Simhendramadhyamam*

p. nata jana paripāla ghana nannu brōvavē

a. śruti moral iḍa lēdā bhū sūtra dhāri nīvē kādā

c. jita manorathulaku mauna yatula tapō niyatulakai
hitamu sēya tanak ahitapu vrātalanu jendina
śrita padambu jīvan āmṛta phalambu nīv ani nā
hitamu pūja viḍanāḍina ataḍē tyāgarāja nuta

Savior of the surrendered devotees,
the Scriptures proclaim

That you are the Master of the Universe.

Knowing that you save all ascetics
and sages, even at a cost to yourself,
I gave up all rituals to focus on you.

Gloss
The Lord is the controller of the destinies of the creatures and, knowing this, Tyagaraja quit his favorite rituals to focus exclusively on meditating on Him. It would appear that the composer is recommending quiet meditation to noisy formal worship, knowing that the saints and liberated sages seek refuge in Him. The last four lines of the song employ *t* rhyme embedded in short syllables. We already know that Tyagaraja recommends bhakti/*jñāna* over karma as a means of gaining Self-Knowledge.

Nenaruncarā nā paini
Raga *Simha Vāhini*

p. nenar uncarā nā paini cāla
nī dāsuḍanu kādā śrī rāma

a. sanak ādi yogi bṛnda vandya pāda
sākēta vāsa sad bhakta pōṣa

c. talli tanḍri guru daivamu nīv ani
tarucugānu ninnu nammi yunna nē
talladilluc unḍa dari jūpav ēmi
tyāgarāja paripāla suguṇa śīla

Look kindly on me, Sri Rama,
Resident of Sāketa and refuge of devotees,
worshipped by sages like Sanaka,
am I not your attendant?

I look on you as my
father, mother, teacher, and God,
yet you don't rescue
a struggling devotee.

Gloss

A simple song without any special poetic devices appeals to the Lord that a devotee who surrenders to Him must be saved.

Nī cittamu nā
Raga *Vijaya Vasanta*

p. nī cittamu nā bhāgyam ayya
nirupādhika nī vāḍan ayya

a. yōcinci kāryamu lēd anucu
oka pāri śaraṇ anukoṇṭin ayya

c. para daivamula jūcinantanē
bhāvam andu nīvē paragedav ayya
dhara lōna nā sarivāralalō
daya jūḍav ayya tyāgarāja nuta

Your grace is my good fortune,
I am yours.

Without hesitation,
I took shelter in you.

When I look at other deities,
I think only of you;
be merciful to me
in the midst of my peers.

Gloss
This is a self-confession on the part of the devotee who is well-established in the Lord and to whom He alone appears in everything (*Bhagavadgita,* 6.29: …the Self abiding in all beings and all beings in the Self—S. Radhakrishnan).

Ninnē bhajana sēyu vāḍanu
Raga *Nāṭa*

p. ninnē bhajana sēyu vāḍanu

a. pannaga śāyi parula vēḍa lēnu

c. snān ādi japa tapa yōga dhyāna
samādhi sukha prada
sītā nātha sakala lōka pālaka
tyāgarāja sannuta

I only worship you
resting on the serpent bed,

I cannot approach other gods—

you render all rituals
like bathing, meditation
and yoga meaningful.

Gloss
Here again Rama's superiority as an easy deity to please and the efficacy of His worship are highlighted. Tyagaraja cast his lot with Him, since any religious observance dedicated to Him produces guaranteed results.

Nitya rūpa evari
Raga *Kāpi*

p. nitya rūpa evari pāṇḍityam ēmi naḍucu rā

a. satyam aina yājña mīra sāmarthyamu kaladā

c. bhānu pagalu rēyi ratna sānu juṭṭaḍā
pūni śeṣuḍ amita bhāra bhūmi mōyaḍā
vīnulandu kāśī pati nī nāmamu palkaḍā
māni tyāgarāja vinuta mahim āspadam agu nī mundu

Eternal Lord,
the highest learning is worthless
weighed against your omnipotence.

None disobeys your rightful law—
the sun orbits the Meru day and night,
the serpent Śesha supports the mighty earth,
The Lord of Kāśī breathes
your holy name in the dying man's ears.

Gloss
One of the common themes across the saint's lyrical corpus is that nothing matches Rama's power, and that nothing violates His law for eternity. This is of course to encourage the devotee to focus his attention all the more on his chosen deity steadfastly. Note that the Kathopanishad also reminds us (II.iii.2.3), "From fear of it (Brahman), fire gives heat. Out of terror, the sun shines. Afraid of it, Indra, Vayu and the fifth, Death, rush to perform their respective duties."
There's the n rhyme in the last four lines of the song in *bhānu, pūni, vīnu,* and *māni.*

Oka pāri jūḍaga
Raga *Kaḷāvati*

p. oka pāri jūḍaga rādā

a śuka mānas ārcita pāda sadā
śuddhāntaranga mudambu tō

c. varul aina dig īśulu candra vibhā-
kara mauni varādulu rāma nī
karuṇā kaṭākṣamu cēta
velasirē kāni tyāgarāja sannuta

O Lord worshipped by Śuka,
would you kindly glance at me once?

The rulers of the quarters,
the sun, the moon, and the sages,
all thrive only through your grace.

Gloss
This is an oblique request to the Lord by the devotee to cast His kind glance in his direction. He will benefit immensely from that. After all, the very gods prosper because of His kindness. There is a slight repetition of the consonant *r* in the last verse. These of course are not regular rhymes, strictly speaking.

Paluku kaṇḍa
Raga *Navarasakannaḍa*

p. paluku kaṇḍa cakkeranu kērunē paṇatulāra jūḍarē

a. koluvu kūṭamunanu kolucu vārini pilici
dāśarathi prēmamīra palikē

c. surula kāminīmaṇula gānam ādaraṇan ālakincucunu
śṛngārarasayukta
vāraramaṇul āḍa jūci sarasa tyāgarājunitōnu pogaḍē

His talk simply is the sweetest there is,
ladies—

The way He addresses His courtiers
full of affection,
as the Demi-gods and goddesses sing and
dance,
and the courtesans display their art of love.

Gloss

Tyagaraja loves to portray Rama as a great savant and patron of arts and letters, while preserving His unique quality of being a charming talker at every turn. Also, it's likely that he is himself fascinated by the court scenes which he describes in such vivid detail.

Parulanu vēḍanu patita
Raga *Balahamsa*

p. parulanu vēḍanu patita pāvanuḍā

a.kari varadā nīvē kānkṣatō brōvum ika

c. amara vara nīdu nām ātiśayambē
jīvanamu sēyuc unnānu śrī tyāgarāja vinuta

I will not seek help from others,
Rama, protector of the destitute,
you help me yourself kindly.

I exist only by the power
of your sacred name.

Gloss

The devotee re-dedicates himself to the Lord and swears loyalty only to Him, the power of whose name sustains him. Lyrics of this type are meant to reinforce the devotee's commitment and strengthen his resolve. The sound *r* appears throughout the lyric; it seems to be one of Tyagaraja's all-time favorites. It has a tendency to roll smoothly off the singer's tongue and please the audience's ears.

Pēriḍi ninu
Raga *Kharaharapriya*

p. pēriḍi ninu pencinavār evarē

a. vārini jūpavē śrī rāmayya

c1. sāra sāratara tāraka nāmamunu

c2. sarva matamulaku sammatamaina

c3. ghōra pātakamula koppuna yaṇacu

c4. tyāgarāju sadā bāguga bhajiyincu

Whoever named you and raised you, Rama,
I'd like to meet them:

The quintessential saving name
that transcends sects
and destroys sin.

Gloss

Since ancient times, the name *Rama* has acquired a special significance as a savior in and of itself. Multiple historical and etymological explanations have been offered for this unique phenomenon where just the name is as powerful as its bearer. Tyagaraja often dwells on its beauty *per se,* thereby instructing the public to take advantage of it, even if people are not capable of other, more demanding spiritual pursuits. If there's a low-hanging fruit on public land, why not pick it?

Rāgaratna mālika cē
Raga *Rītigauḷa*

p. rāga ratna mālikacē ranjillun aṭa hari śata

a. bāga sēvinci sakala bhāgyam andudāmu rārē

c. naigama ṣaṭ śāstra purāṇ āgamārtha sahitam aṭa
yōgi varulu ānandamun ondē san mārgam aṭa
bhāgavat ōttamulu kūḍi pāḍē kīrtanamul aṭa
tyāgarāju kaḍatēra tārakam ani cēsina śata

Sri Hari delights in the diamond
necklaces of ragas,
so let's sing His glory together
and be blessed by Him.

They distill the essence

of the Vedas and the Scriptures,
they are adopted by yogis
wherefrom they derive immense joy,
and are sung by the greatest devotees;
they were composed by Tyagaraja
for his own redemption.

Gloss

This song is significant in that Tyagaraja comes out and declares that music is an established way of pleasing the Lord and that he composed his songs as a means of liberation. Toward the end of his life, he was conducting biweekly *bhajans* at the temple, just as he recommends in this song. So the ultimate goal of his compositions is liberation. This has been his objective all along. He never wanted to cater to the vainglory of kings or other dignitaries, though he risked his well-being by doing so.

Rakṣa peṭṭarē
Raga *Bhairavi*

p. rakṣa peṭṭarē doraku

a. vakṣasthalamuna velayu lakṣmī ramaṇuniki sāya

c. sītā karamunu paṭṭi celagina doraku
vātātmajuniki ceyi vaśamaina doraku
puruhūtādula rakṣimpa bāhujudaina doraku
sangīta priya tyāgarāja gēyudaina dorakaiśvarya

May this amulet protect at dusk
the Lord with Lakshmi on his chest,

the Lord who married Sita
and whom Hanuman readily accesses.

who offers protection to Indra and the gods
and is worshipped by Tyagaraja.

Gloss

At the end of all religious rituals in India it is customary to sing the praises of the deity just worshipped and wish the deity well. Not that God needs man's benediction, but it is used as a form of prayer, 'All the best to the Lord,' *'te bhavatu maṅgalam.'*

Rāma kathā
Raga *Madhyamāvati*

p. rāma kathā sudhā rasa pānamoka rājyamu jēsunē

a. bhāmāmaṇi jānaki saumitri bharatādulatō bhūmi velayu śrī

c. dharmādyakhila phaladamē manasā
dhairyānanda saukhya nikētanamē
karma bandha jvalanābdhi nāvamē
kaliharamē tyāgarāja vinutuḍagu

Imbibing the elixir of the story of Rama

attended upon by Sita, Lakshmana, and Bharata
is like gaining a kingdom.
It results from of the study of scriptures,
grants bliss, hope, and happiness,

and ferries you across the waters of karma.

Gloss

Recounting the stories of gods and saints is considered auspicious in itself. The saints themselves sang the glories of the Lord, and we humans continue the tradition. Tyagaraja here encourages us to immerse ourselves in the chanting of the traditional accounts of Rama to redeem ourselves and qualify for His mercy.

Rāmābhirāma manasu ranjilla
Raga *Dhanyāsi*

p. rām ābhirāma manasu ranjilla palaka rādā

a. ī mahini velasinad ēmi sadā nātō

c. bangāru mēṭi pānpupai bhāmā maṇi jānaki
śṛngārincukoni celuv onda ninnu kani
pongucu malle virula pūjincu vēḷa śrī hari
sangītamu pāḍum ani svāmi tyāgarājunitō

O Rama, speak with me
and gladden my heart,
having incarnated in the world.

Tell me to sing for you,
As Sita, the gracious lady,
decked out and beaming,
offers you jasmines in worship.

Gloss
In any number of his songs, Tyagaraja requests favours of the Lord after making sure Sita is present and He is in a good mood. Sometimes, he asks Sita to mediate disputes or to plead his case with Him. This is not merely good psychology, but an acknowledgment of the fact that the Lord and His Consort are one and the same and that asking one for a favour is the same as appealing to both simultaneously. Sometimes, the scene gets crowded with his brothers and Hanuman too in attendance. Another thing, Tyagaraja here specifically offers to sing for Rama for his own delight. After all, the purpose of his songs and music is the exaltation of his mind and its decoupling from the world.

Sangīta jñānamu
Raga *Dhanyāsi*

p. sangīta jñānamu bhakti vinā sanmārgamu kaladē manasā

a. bhṛngi naṭēśa samīraja ghaṭaja matanga nāradādul upāsincē

c. nyāyānyāyamu telusunu
jagamulu māyāmayamani telusunu
durguṇa kāyajādi ṣadripula jayincu kāryamu
telusunu tyāgarājuniki

Mastery of music sans devotion
cannot be the proper path to Realization—
music adored by the saints.

The real musician can tell

the moral from the immoral,
that the world is illusory,
and how to counteract
the destructive sensory tendencies.

Gloss

In several songs, Tyagaraja mentions his idea of the purpose of music and how it is enhanced by the devotional sentiment. In other words, he believed that there should be a guiding *bhāva* to inspire grand music. That *bhāva* for him was liberation through bhakti, expressed in a musical idiom. There's never any doubt as to where he is coming from in each and every one of his lyrics. To Tyagaraja bhakti is the same as the Lord's bliss, the Self of the *advaitin,* that is to be sought after.

Sangīta śāstra jñānamu
Raga *Mukhāri*

p. sangīta śāstra jñanamu
sārūpya saukhyadamē manasā

a. śṛngāra rasād yakhila sāra
pūrita rāma kath ānand ābdhi yuta

c. prēma bahkti sujana vātsalyamu
śrīmad ramā vara kaṭakṣamu
nēma niṣṭha yaśō dhanam osangunē
nērpu kalgu tyāgarāju nērcina

Knowledge of music
takes me closer to the form of the Lord,

when combined with
all the sentiments embedded
in the joyous story of Rama;

Love, devotion,
blessings of the holy,
the Lord's grace, self-control,
and renown will then follow.

Gloss

Here's another grand declaration that music along with the depiction of the literary sentiments that the story of Rama incorporates in itself will help the devotee identify himself with His divine form. Furthermore, music with all its components, notably the lyric that conveys those sentiments, will foster in the devotee the attributes of pure love and self-control that prepare him for the grace of the Lord. Note that, among the four stages of spiritual progress, *sārūpya* or identity of form is the first one that paves the way to *sāyujya* or merger in the Godhead. Sankara in *Śivānandalaharī (28)* says that *sārūpya* can be attained through the Lord's worship (*pūjane)* when the devotee will be immersed in the ritual to the point where he forgets his own identity.

Śara śara samaraika
Raga *Kuntala Varāḷi*

p. śara śara samar aika śūra
śaradhi mada vidāra

a. sura ripu mūla balam anu
tūla girulak anala samamau śrī rāma

c. toli jēsina pāpa vana kuṭhāramā
kalan ainanu sēyaga lēni
balu viluni virici velasina śrī raghu
kula vara brōvumu tyāgarāja nuta

O Warrior who deployed
a leaf of grass as an arrow,
and who subdued the ocean,

you are an ember to the
demons' hills of cotton fiber,

you are the saber that lays flat
the dense forest of my past sins,
you did the unimaginable feat
of shattering the bow,

please show me your grace.

Gloss
A prayer to the all-powerful Lord to shed His grace on the devotee. The idea is that for the Almighty who accomplished so much, it should not be hard to save one more supplicant. This song was likely inspired by the British drum beats à la the Western style of Muttuswami Dikshitar.

Sari yevvarē śrī jānaki
Raga *Śrī Rañjani*

p. sari yevvarē śrī jānaki nī

a. paramātmunikai gaḍitēri sadā

sirul iccuṭaku cēri kolicina nī

c. vanam andu bhayankaram aina
tāvuna niltun ani manasu telisi
kanakāngi yand anduna rāja sukhambunu
kalga jēsitivē tyāgarāja nutē

O Mother Janaki,
no one's comparable to you.

Coming into existence for the Supreme Lord,
you are ever ready to bestow your grace
on one and all.

You provided the comforts of the palace
in the middle of the forest
knowing the Lord's mind

Gloss

In one of several lyrics in praise of Sita, the saint says that She is unequaled for two reasons: She grants everybody' wishes, and Her devotion to Her consort is such that She recreated the whole palace in the middle of nowhere. A simple and elegant offering to Sita, Tyagaraja having designed it that way with a short song. The beauty of this song derives from the stark contrast between the fierce forest and the opulent palace.

Sītamma mā yamma
Raga *Vasanta*

p. sītamma māyamma śrīrāmuḍu māku tanḍri

a. vātātmaja saumitri vainatēya ripu mardana
dhāta bharat ādulu sōdarulu māku manasā

c. paramēśa vasiṣṭha parāśara nārada śaunaka śuka
surapati gautama lambōdara guha sanak ādulu
dhara nija bhāgavat āgrēsarul evarō vār ellaru
vara tyāgarājuniki parama bāndhavulu manasā

Sita is our mother, Rama our father,

Hanuman, Lakshmana, Garuda,
Śatrughna, Brahma, and Bharata
are brothers to us, O Mind.

Sages Narada, Śaunaka, and Sanaka,
and all other dedicated devotees
are our close kinsmen, O Mind.

Gloss
The devotee feels that not only are Rama and Sita his parents, but the members of their family as well, even as every established devotee is his kinsman. That helps him identify himself as part of the Lord's family and therefore feel blessed. It's a way of reinforcing his conviction that the Lord belongs to him and he to the Lord. The *caranam* displays the *r* rhyme, Tyagaraja's favorite. The first three lines rhyme the letter t.

Sogasu jūda taramā
Raga *Kannaḍagauḷa*

p. sogasu jūḍa taramā nī

a. niganigamanucu sukapōlayugamucē merayu mōmu

c1. amarārcita padayugamu abhayaprada karayugamu
kamanīya tanu nindita kāma kāmaripu nuta nī

c2. vara bimba samādharamu vakuḷa sumambula yuramu
karadhṛta śara kōdaṇḍa marakatānga varamaina

c3. cirunagavulu mungurulu mari kannula tēṭayu
vara tyāgarāja vandanīya yiṭuvanṭi

Your handsome features are sublime:

your shiny cheeks lighting up the face,
with feet worshipped by the gods,
hands blessing the humanity,
and looks putting the love-god to shame;

your nether lip is like the bimba fruit,
your chest adorned by fragrant *vakula* blooms,
and bow and arrows by the blue diamond body;

your face resplendent with lovely locks and smiles,
and eyes clear as crystal pools.
You are truly praiseworthy.

Gloss

Notice the contrast between the two depictions of Sita and Rama. They are glaring in their length and diversity. Sita gets a couple of lines and Rama at least twelve. *But* there is no qualitative difference, in that the lyricist packs the same amount of punch in both songs, which only a consummate artist can do. While Rama's body is radiant, Sita's loving concern for Him and Her devotees is extraordinary.

Sogasugā mṛdanga tāḷamu
Raga *Śrī Rañjani*

p. sogasugā mṛdanga tāḷamu jata kūrci ninu
sokka jēyu dhīruḍ evvaḍō

a. nigama śirōrthamu kalgina
nija vākkulatō svara śuddhamutō

c. yati viśrama sad bhakti
virati drākṣā rasa nava rasa
yuta kṛticē bhajiyincu
yukti tyāgarājuni taramā

Can anyone truly delight you
with their music to match
the beat of drums?

With words replete with Vedic
vibrations and perfect notes,

woven into a *kṛti* exuding
the nine sentiments with
appropriate pauses
and interlinked sounds?

Tyagaraja is no match.

Gloss
In this unique lyric, Tyagaraja describes the entire science, philosophy, and technique of making a *kṛti.* All its components are laid out, including essentially the Vedic connotations of the *sāhitya,* without which there is no lyric or its accompanying music. In fact, this lyric characterizes, better than we ever could, our entire work here!

Śrī rāma pādamā
Raga *Amṛtavāhini*

p. śrī rāma pādamā nī kṛpa cālunē cittāniki rāvē

a. vārija bhava sanaka sanandana vāsavādi nāradulella pūjincē

c. dārini śilayai tāpamu tāḷaka
vāramu kannīrunu rālcaga
śūra ahalyanu jūci brōcitivi
ā rīti dhanyu sēyavē tyāgarāja gēyamā

Holy foot of Rama,
come dwell in my mind.
The sages all worshipped you.

On the roadway, you noticed
a stone and transformed it
into Ahalya, relieving her misery.

Gloss
Tyagaraja sings the glory of the Lord's feet and their unique power. Worshipped by the sages, the holy foot has the unique distinction of having transformed the petrified Ahalya back into

a woman. He requests the same grace for himself whereby he would be redeemed.

Śrī rāma rāma jagadātma
Raga *Pūrṇacandrika*

p. śrī rāma rāma jagadātma rāma
śrī rāma raghurāma pāhi paramātma

c1. jyōtirmayākhaṇḍa rūpa rāma
bhūtēśa vinutāpahṛta bhakta tāpa

c2. sarva grah ādhārabhūta rāma
gīrvāṇa muni vandya sujanēṣṭadāta

c3. yōgijana hṛdayābja mitra rāma
bhōgi śāyi ghṛṇārasa pūrṇa nētra

c4. śrī dānta śānta nirvāṇa phalada
vēdānta vēdy āvanīsura trāṇa

c5. tvām vinā nānyatra jānē rāma
tvām vinā kō gatir jānakī jānē

c6. dhīra bhava sāgarōttaraṇa rāma
sāratara śrī tyāgarāja nuta caraṇa

O Rama, the World Soul,
and the Supreme Soul,
show mercy to me.

Resplendent in form, and praised by the gods,
you free devotees from all misery,

you are the support of all planets,
and are worshipped by the divine sages;

the yogis bask in your effulgence,
you who rest on the serpent bed,
with eyes brimming with compassion;

you grant the wishes of everyone
including liberation,
you are the saviour of the learned and the
pious;

I know no other Lord,
and have no other refuge,
O consort of Janaki;
You are my ferry across the ocean of samsara.

Gloss

This song is included here for two reasons: it's in Sanskrit, and it directly addresses Rama as the Universal Self. The gravity of the *bhāva* inspires its expression in Sanskrit. Furthermore, every couplet of the lyric employs rhyme in the service of sound effects and its overall memorability. The raga *Purnacandrika* is particularly suited to the lyric and keeps the military rhythm reverberating in the audience's minds long after they have heard it.

Suguṇamulē ceppukonṭi
Raga *Cakravākam*

p. suguṇamulē ceppukonṭi
sundara raghu rāma

a. vagal erungalēka yiṭu
vattuv anucu durāsacē

c. snān ādi sukarmambulu
vēd ādhyayanambul eruga
śrī nāyaka kṣamiyincumu
śrī tyāgarāja nuta

I only keep recounting your merits
hoping I could see you,
and not knowing your guiles.

Forgive me if I haven't
Done any ritual worship
or studied the Scriptures.

Gloss

In a negative sort of way, Tyagaraja is saying that it is enough to read the story of Rama and contemplate His virtues, in order to qualify for His grace. He makes bhakti sound so easy that there is no excuse for anyone not to become an instant devotee.

Sukhiyevarō
Raga *Kānaḍa*

p. sukhiyevarō rāma nāma sukhiyevarō

a. sukhiyevarō sumukhiyevarō akhila sāramagu tāraka nāma

c. satyamu tappaga sakala lōkulaku bhṛtyuḍai daiva bhēdamu lēka

nityamaina susvarapu gānamutō nirantaramu
tyāgarāja nuta nāma

The happy person enjoying the bliss
of Rama's potent name is gracious,
he lives a pure and truthful life
ever for the sake of his fellow-men
regardless of religion,
singing beautiful music in perpetuity.

Gloss

The most important notion expressed in this short song occurs in the third line of the stanza, namely that the happiest person on earth is one who dwells in the Lord regardless of sectarian considerations. Then of course that person is selfless.

Tulasī daḷamulacē
Raga *Māyāmāḷavagauḷa*

p. tulasī daḷamulacē santōṣamugā pūjintu

a. palumāru cira kālamu paramātmuni pādamulanu

c. sarasīruha punnāga campaka pāṭala kuravaka
karavīra mallikā sugandha rāja sumamul
dharan ivi yoka paryāyamu dharm ātmuni sākēta
pura vāsuni śrī rāmuni vara tyāgarāja nutuni

I will happily worship the Lord's feet
With leaves of the holy basil
over and over again for long,

along with fragrant flowers from every bush.

He is Sri Rama, the dweller of Saketa,
the blameless Lord.

Gloss

While Tyagaraja ritualistically worshipped Sri Rama every day, in this song he expresses the desire to perform a special *pūjā* to His feet with the leaves of the *tulasī* bush for greater satisfaction and benefit. After the first line, *r* is the predominant sound in the rest of the lyric.

Upacāramu jēsēvār unnārani
Raga *Bhairavi*

p. upacāramu jēsēvar unnārani maravakurā

a. kṛpa kāvalen ani nē nī
kīrtini palkucun unḍaga

c. vākiṭanē padilamugā vātātmajuḍ unnāḍ ani
śrī karul agu nī tammulu cēri yunnār ani
ēkāntamunanu jānaki yērpaḍi yunnad ani
śrī kānta parulēl ani śrī tyāgarāja vinuta

Please don't forget
there are others who are
waiting to serve you,
though Hanuman is at the door,
your brothers at your service,
and Sita keeps you company
in private;

as I sing your glory
and seek your mercy.

Gloss
Tyagaraja knows when Rama is with his family, and wants to wait his turn singing the Lord's praises. Besides, Hanuman wouldn't let him in, anyway.

The song is another way of appealing to the Lord so that He would not forget him as He is already well-served by His family and Hanuman.

Vēr evvarē gati
Raga *Suraṭi*

p. vēr evvarē gati vēmārulaku sītā pati

a. īrēḍu lōkamulak ādhāruḍ agu ninnu vinā

c. bṛndārak ādi muni bṛnda śuka sanaka
sanandana śrī nārad āravindōdbhava śrī bhava
purandarulaku tyāgarājuniki ninnu vinā

O Consort of Sita,
Who is the support of the fourteen
worlds, and all the sages
and devotees like Śuka, Sanaka,
Sanandana, Narada, Indra,
and Tyagaraja other than you?

Gloss

The devotee likes to remind himself of his origins and his support during his life. Tyagaraja does it frequently in his compositions in different ways. This is one of those reinforcing statements by Tyagaraja. The last three lines have the plesant *-nda-* combination of sounds.

Afterword

As we conclude the *Companion,* we get a tremendous sense of satisfaction that the *sāhitya* (textual) aspect of Tyagaraja's monumental work has, at the very least, been addressed and the awareness of his lyrical skills has been raised among his admirers. Needless to say, a lot more can be done, and more of his songs can be included in further studies. We hope that a fresh venue of the appreciation—and understanding—of the saint's literary skills has been opened. It's not just another aspect of the study of his work: it is *the* analysis of his *geyas* as clues to his approach to the Lord. In any case, the infinite variety of the devices used in his poetry is itself rewarding to analyze and study. I daresay that he almost *weaponized* the lyric in his struggle for salvation. Other kinds of textual analyses are possible.

We have not touched Tyagaraja's divine music, its novelty, and its sheer pleasure—aspects that have been thoroughly studied by musical scholars.

Appendix

Tyagaraja and the Targeted Lyric,
article published in Mountain Path, Oct 2019, by kind permission.

Sudha Emany[1]

Tyagaraja's[2] *modus operandi* was bhakti; his ultimate target was *mukti*. His musical compositions (as well as his life) bear ample testimony to this observation.

Interestingly—and indubitably—the former is a surefire way of achieving the latter. As explained by Bhagavan Ramana Maharshi,[3]

> *Bhakti* is not different from *mukti*. *Bhakti* is being as the Self (*swarupa)*. One is always that. He realizes it by the means he adopts. What is *bhakti?* To think of *God*. That means only one thought prevails to the exclusion of all other thoughts. That thought is of God which is the Self or it is the self surrendered unto God. When He has taken you up nothing will assail. The absence of thought is *bhakti*. It is also *mukti*.

The consummate singer Swami Vivekananda, in his "Addresses on Bhaktiyoga," says that in ancient India "music and dance...are essentially religious in character and were used as a means of expressing devotion to and realizing

---

[1] Sudha Emany, M.A. (English), Dip. in Sanskrit, Dip. in Violin, has taught (teaches) at the Vivekananda Institute of Languages, Ramakrishna Math, Hyderabad. This article is a digest of her upcoming book *Tyagaraja: Lyric to Liberation, A Story Retold* (Delhi: Motilal Banarsidass, 2019).

[2] 1767-1847

[3] *Talks with Sri Ramana Maharshi,* Three volumes in one, 10th ed. (Tiruvannamalai: Sri Ramanasramam, 1996). p. 611.

God."[4] He then describes the requirements of a successful concert:[5]

> Assuming that the voice of the singer is sweet, good, and correctly tuned instruments...will undoubtedly increase the total effect. The whole concert will get a polished touch if the science and technique of music are suitably combined.
>
> All this combination will be to no purpose *if the composition that is sung is not sufficiently poetical and is bereft of fine noble sentiments. If a really good composition is sung with feeling and in sufficiently clear tones so as to bring out the correct meaning and sentiments contained in it, the total effect will be marvelous.*
> (Italics mine)

These brief remarks by Vivekananda contain the *totality* of ingredients of great music and a successful performance, viz. sweet voice, properly tuned instruments, original technique, sincerity of feeling, *and meaning and sentiment.*

This article focuses on the last ingredient—the poetry and the nobility of sentiment in music, as delineated in the lyrics of the Carnatic musician and saint Tyagaraja and will see how it achieves the dual aim of music, of "devotion to and realizing God," noted by Vivekananda above.

Targeted Lyrics

Arguably, it is this ability of Tyagaraja's directing his lyrics at specific persons, places, and things that gave him a slight edge over the two other members of the Trinity, Syāma Sastri and Muthuswami Dīkṣitar.[6] Every one of Tyagaraja's songs was context-based and composed to address a specific life situation.

---

[4] Harshananda, "Music and Vivekananda," *Vedanta Kesari,* January 1965. p. 467. Online.

[5] *Ibid.*

[6] Syama Sastri, 1762-1827; Dikshitar, 1775-1835.

This is the major reason for the perfect fit of his language to his music. His lyrics ennobled his music, even as his music energized his lyrics.

Tyagaraja was not just another musician. Neither was he just a composer. He was equal parts composer, singer, *and* saint. The spiritual fragrance emanating straight from his heart and expressed musically in his lyrics set him firmly on the road to liberation. Not all musical writing can claim the same puissance, and neither do all composers who practice their craft primarily to please themselves care to be dropped at the doorstep of *mokṣa.*

Professor V. Raghavan, in his Preface to *The Spiritual Heritage of Tyagaraja*, observes:[7]

> Tyagaraja was both a devotee and an artist; the combination of Vedanta, devotion and literary treatment in his songs naturally reminded one of the Bhagavata Purana…

The primacy of *sāhitya* in music was hinted at as long ago as Valmiki's day in the *śloka* making obeisance to him: *kūjantaṁ rāma rāmeti madhuraṁ madhurākṣaram/āruhya kavitā śākhāṁ vande vālmīki kokilam.* For Valmiki the *kokila* to sing, the melodious word *Rāma* was needed. Or it was as good as silent! The repetitive use of the epithet *madhura* leaves no doubt about the sweetness of the melody being intensified when the syllables *rā* and *mā* were sung, preferably in that order. Thus both the lexis and syntax of the lyric are showcased in music.

Tyagaraja's chosen path to attain to the Divine was destined to lie through his music and his devotion to Rama, both of which depended on his lyrical prowess. He bared his soul to the Lord through the innovative singing of his unique lyrics. His innermost feelings were laid at the feet of his Lord in the form

---

[7] C. Ramanujachari, *The Spiritual Heritage of Tyagaraja* (Mylapore, Madras: Ramakrishna Math, 2001). p. iii.

of unheard-of melodies. The man was the same as his *bhāva*[8], which was explored through his lyrics. His *bhāva* led him to his Lord and to his liberation, when it matured into renunciation and identification with Him.

The Many Concepts of Bhakti

Bhakti is the overarching target that Tyagaraja aimed his lyrics at. Any number of his lyrics extol the importance of bhakti as well as the incomparable happiness that a devotee derives from it. Besides the time-honored definitions of bhakti by Narada[9] and Sandilya,[10] we have a pragmatic description of it by Sankara[11]:

> That state of mind is called Bhakti (divine love) wherein all movements of thought go automatically to the lotus feet of the Lord and stick to them forever just as the seed of Ankola tree (on falling) gravitates to the parent tree, the iron needle to the magnetic stone, the devoted wife to her husband, the creeper to the tree and the river to the ocean.

Under the rubric of bhakti, we have a number of subcategories or subtargets. According to Narada, bhakti can take any one of eleven different modes: glorification of the Lord's qualities; attachment to His beauty, His worship, or His reminiscence; attachment as a servant to his master (*dāsya)*; as a friend (*sneha)*; as a parent to his son (*vātsalya),* or as a wife to her husband (*madhura);* total surrender to Him *(śaraṇāgati);*

---

[8] A very powerful term referring to the deepest sentiments felt by a writer, composer, or singer.

[9] *Narada Bhakti Sutras,* 2. Tr. Swami Bhuteshananda (Calcutta: Advaita Ashrama, 1990). *sā tasmin parama prema svarūpā.* Bhakti is of the nature of supreme love for the Lord.

[10] *Śandilya Bhakti Sutras,* I.1.2. *sā parānuraktir īśvare,* quoted by Radhakrishnan, p. 60, fn. Bhakti is supreme love for the Lord.

[11] *Śivānandalaharī or Inundation of Divine Bliss of Srī Śankarācārya,* Tr. Swami Tapasyananda (Mylapore, Madras: Sri Ramakrishna Math, 1985). Verse 61, pp. 55-56.

complete absorption in Him *(sārūpya);* and extreme anguish due to separation from Him.[12]

Additional targets that the saint covered—and he covered any number of them—include: knowledge *(jñāna)* and *renunciation (vairagya),* which have their own subtargets of contempt for money and possessions, association with good people, desirelessness, and eschewing the company of wicked people. Furthermore, the saint also referred frequently to the "six enemies" within (*ari ṣaḍvarga)*[13] and the three *guṇas.*[14]

Due to limitations of space, we will try to illustrate here only the major nuances of bhakti that the saint dealt with in his lyrics with one or two examples each.

It is clear from his compositions in all contexts, generally speaking, that Tyagaraja constantly aimed at inculcating *jñāna* and indifference to the world and its erroneous ways. In fact, it may be the conscious teaching that he emphasized that, regardless of the turbulence that constantly buffets the world, an individual can transcend its impact by leading a spiritual life, and the Lord is sure to provide succor to them.

The idiom he used was contemporary. The Telugu dialect that he drew upon was his own. He freely used a mix of Sanskritized lexical items, spoken as well as written vocabulary, and on occasion even obscure words. The combination must have been effective during his time and immediately after but, over time, some of the usages might appear a bit odd. But there has never been a diminution of the overall effect; the lyrics are as powerful today as the day they were written, and the appeal to the Lord as direct.

---

[12] *Narada Bhakti Sutras,* Tr. Swami Bhuteshananda (Calcutta: Advaita Ashrama, 1990). pp. 190-192.

[13] *kāma* (desire), *krodha* (anger), *lobha* (greed), *moha* (attachment, including physical attraction), *mada* (arrogance), and *mātsarya* (envy).

[14] *sattva* (serenity), *rajas* (passion), and *tamas* (ignorance, dullness).

Tyagaraja never sat down on a fine morning and decided to write songs. The creative afflatus was constantly with him. He just composed and sang his songs impromptu when he felt the urge to do so. His disciples then recorded both the lyric and the music while he was immersed in the Divine. All his songs and their music were spontaneous, having been an instant response to specific emotional impulses.

In the following examples of the lyrics, immediately following the translated text, the raga and the first words are given in parentheses. The original songs, with annotations, are available online. The "translations" are meant to convey the *bhāva* of each *kṛti* in user-friendly English and are not word-for-word renderings.

Tyagaraja might have honed his literary and poetic skills with his Sanskrit compositions, his very first composition being in Sanskrit. One of his perennially popular songs praises Krishna as he plays tantalizing music on his magic flute. Its brief import is:

O Lord with the stately bearing of an elephant—

the Lord who exhilarates the hearts of sages
who is beyond time,
who is the master of music that emanates from the Vedas,
who is merciful
who is the eternal Om made up of the seven notes
who is born in the house of Yadus, who plays the magic flute—

please take care of me.

(Hindolam, *sāmaja vara gamana)*

The popularity of the song however depends on the Sanskrit original and its linguistic features:

the preponderance of the mellifluous *m* and *l*, the alternation of long and short syllables controlling the tempo, the series of long *ā* sounds throughout the song, and the prevalence of *d* in the last verse. The net effect is a leisurely trochaic[15] movement of the song, giving the audience time to soak in the meaning. Note that the very first word of the song, *sāmaja,* refers to an elephant, a term which evokes a stately, measured gait. The rest of the song elaborates the theme of sustained devotion to the Lord who plays haunting music made up of the seven notes derived from the Vedas.

It would seem that, since Sanskrit was dubbed a classical language not widely used by the general public by his day, he was trying to make up for that handicap with features like rhyme, sound effects, systematic alternation of long and short syllables, and select sounds designed to produce a specific *rasa*. This particular song fulfills all those requirements splendidly.

A prime example of the composer's craftsmanship is the first of the *pancha ratnas* (the "Five Gems"), *jagadānandakāraka,* in which the vocabulary, metaphors, sound effects, and connotations coalesce into a magnificent structure. There are some over a hundred instances of the sound *r,* which gives the song its characteristic lilting cadence. The next most used phoneme is probably *n/ṇ*. Also short vowels seem to heavily outnumber the long ones, giving the song a somewhat strident movement, but it is the opposition of the short and long vowels that maintains the tension in the song throughout. The other obvious feature of the work is its long compounds spilling over the musical phrases deliberately. The tempo evokes the majestic trot of an Arabian horse with a perfect rhythm. And then there is a contiguity of slow and fast movements. The net result of the combination of these and other features is that the

---

[15] A trochee is the reverse of an iamb, and is a foot consisting of a long and a short syllable in poetry (accented and unaccented in English.

listener is immersed in esthetic joy, *rasa,* the more immediate *ānanda* than the spiritual one.

Tyagaraja not only transfers these tools to his Telugu compositions but adds, augments, and modifies them in myriad ways. In one song, he lists the various ways in which the devotee can worship his Lord.

Refuge of the sinful, life of the pure,
Won't you speak to me and show your grace to me,

As I show fortitude, hide my distress,
wail, or wise up,

meditate on you, worship you,
adore you, and beckon to you

behold you, sing your praises,
subdue my pride, treasure you in my heart

hold on to you, scold you,
and lay myself down at your feet

sport with you, sing about you,
beg you, and adulate you

seek sanctuary with you,
and scold you

comprehend you, agree with you
tire of looking for you, learn about your name

greet you, or be grabbed by you,
and exhausted, submit to you?

(Ārabhi, *palukavemi patita pāvana)*

Since the basis of all these modes of serving the Lord is bhakti, he begs Him to grant him unwavering devotion in a short lyric:

O Rama, I beg you to grant me
bhakti of the highest order,

that which lies behind the power
of the Trinity and freedom from bondage.

For learning of the Vedas and epics
without it is like decorating a corpse.

(Śankarābharaṇam, *bhakti biccamiyyave)*

Morality

A powerful current of thought that undergirds the whole of Tyagaraja's life, devotion, and work is morality and ethics. He is convinced that, without a moral basis, human life is a total waste. It is almost criminal not to make the best use of the invaluable opportunity that human life provides to help others and to evolve to the next level, getting ever closer to the Divine. Given that humans are rational beings, they have the choice: to grow into the Divine, or wallow in the mud like swine.

But even to resist the tendency to engage in unethical and immoral activity, one needs the grace of the Lord. Tyagaraja was well aware of that and in many of his songs explicitly asks for true knowledge:

Would you kindly impart true knowledge to me.

My mind is purified by the repetition of your name—

The knowledge that the individual self and the Supreme Self,
the fourteen worlds, the celestials, and sages like Narada
are all you, perfect and whole, the source of endless joy.

(Pūrvikalyāṇi, *jñānamosagarādā)*

For those who are unable to devote themselves full time to activities related to ritual worship, there is even a simpler way to happiness, namely, the repetition of His name:

To those who have a human form,
repeating the name is itself joy,

to those who are rāja yogis.

By hearing Rama's name,
One's mind is filled with His form
and love for Him.

(Janaranjani, *smaraṇe sukhamu)*

The best way to understand Tyagaraja's moral instruction is as a kind of friendly advice rather than a harangue from on high. He laments the ostentation of people for the sake of eking out a living and getting ahead in the world, without at least trying to consider what a life of devotion is—and what knowledge is, if possible. He is clearly puzzled by human nature that acts as a barrier to understanding itself and its origins. How could anyone forget who they are and where they and the world came from? Worse still, how could they not see the path of devotion to the Lord that lies right in front of his eyes? Delusion worse deluded!

O Mind,

There is but one God, Rāma,
don't distract yourself—

within the orb of the sun
one devoid of qualities,
He is dharma,
impartial and just,
the protector of all.

(Harikāmbhoji, *uṇḍedi rāmuḍokaḍu)*

Mind, the Monkey

The next song presents a bare-knuckles approach to the wandering mind, without first controlling which no amount of *sadhana* does a scintilla of good. The first two lines of the last verse below deliberately provoke humor at the expense of the ritualists.

If the mind is not steady,
impressive worship is useless.

If a self-conceited person
takes a holy bath in the Kaveri or the Ganga,
the river cannot save him.

The ritualist
cannot qualify for heaven,
if his spouse is attracted to other men.
If the angry or lustful one
practices austerities,
he will not be saved.

(Ābhogi, *manasu nilpa)*

Mind is not an easy-to-grasp concept. Bhagavan provides a very clear picture of the elusive mind and its antics:[16]

> The mind is only a force operating on the brain. You are now here and awake. The thoughts of the world and the surroundings are in the brain within the body...The dream visions are in the dream brain which is again in the dream body. That is different from your present body. You remember the dream now. The brains however are different. Yet the visions appear in the mind. The mind therefore is not

[16] *Talks with Sri Ramana Maharshi.* Page numbers are in parentheses.

> identical with the brain. Waking, dream and sleep are for the mind only. (455-6)
>
> Tyagaraja says well. The mind should be controlled. The question arises "What is mind?" He (Tyagaraja) himself answers in the next couplet saying that it is the "I-am-the-body" idea. The next question is how the control is effected. He answers again, saying "By complete surrender. Realise that I am not and that all is He." The song is fine and compact. (418).

Here's the song that Bhagavan was talking about:

The wise one who has his senses under control
has no need of mantra or mysticism.

One who knows that he is not the body has no need of austerities.

One who knows that the Lord pervades all has no stages of life.
One who knows that objects are a delusion is not fooled by female charm.

One who forever follows right conduct has no fear of birth and death.

(Śankarābharaṇam, *manasu svādhīnamaina)*

Reproachful Devotion

Tyagaraja did not hesitate to play the blame game when it suited his purpose:

O Rama,

It's not nice to ignore those
who put their trust in you.

It's unfair to abandon those
who from their early days have
thought only of you,
served and worshipped you,
fixed your form in their hearts,
and sang your praises,
even while engaged in the world.

(Bhairavi, *nammina vārini)*

He questions the Lord whether He hasn't seen enough of his public humiliation:

Haven't you seen enough already,
or do you need to see more?

Is there a sin that cannot be erased by you?

Not worshipping your feet,
I was lured by greed and snared by the world.

Those who are not afraid to sin
envied my conduct;
I cannot take it anymore,
I have taken refuge at your holy feet.
Fount of Mercy, no one other than you
can provide me succor.

(Śankarābharaṇam, *īvaraku jūcinadi cāladā)*

Sensuous Love *(Madhura Bhakti)*

When Rama asked Hanuman the ideal devotee what he thought his relationship to Him was, Hanuman said that, viewed as an individual, he was His servant; as a living entity, he originated from Him; as a deathless soul, he was the same as Him.[17] A perfect answer if ever there was one from a *jñāni* of a very high order.

On an earthly level, *Madhura Bhakti* is a tricky but time-honored variety of self-surrender to the *Purusha,* the Cosmic Man, a genre celebrated in the Radha-Krishna narratives and in the pining of the shepherdesses for Krishna. The latter is explained as the fulfillment of the desire of accomplished sages in a former era for union with the Divine—the eternal quest of the *jīvātman* to return to its source whence it originated, *Paramātman.*[18]

We encounter here some very haunting compositions, in a familiar conversational tone of voice:

> *Whose prattle have you listened to,*
> *O Lord of Ayodhya, praised by the great sages?*
>
> *You don't talk to me like before,*
> *You have changed.*
>
> (Śuddha sāveri, *nīkevari bodhana)*

In another song, the lover employs a different tactic, one of blaming her fate, in a self-deprecatory fashion, for best impact:

> *O Rama, with an enchanting name,*
> *brave as a lion, and living in Ayodhya!*
>
> *I am tired of waiting for you,*
> *no point in complaining.*
>
> *My mind, your sweetheart, is pining for you,*
> *but you don't hold her hand and solace her.*

---

[17] *deha buddhyātu dāso'ham, jīva buddhyā tvadaṁśakaḥ/ātmabuddhyā tvamevāham iti me niścitā matiḥ.*
[18] *Brahma Sutra,* I.i.2. *janmādyasya yataḥ.*

I worship and worship you,
but it's my fate that I am ignored by you.

I made a lovely bed for you,
without enjoying which you heckle me.

(Darbār, *rāmābhirāma ramaṇīya nāma)*

The Ultimate Target: The Self

Tyagaraja the lyricist never once strayed from his ultimate target, the Self. This song may be said to be in the back of his mind from day one.

O lovely blue-tinged Lord,

O radiant Rāmachandra,

Destroyer of demons, dwelling in the hearts of yogis,

You are all the gods yourself on earth

I am fond of you, and I am not other than you!

(Dhanyāsi, *śyāma sundarāṅga*)

He thought of Rama when he was awake; he dreamt of Him when asleep; and when he worshipped Him, he became one with Him. He nevertheless wished to formally renounce the world and become a *sannyasin* toward the end of his life. Making himself the final target of his own lyrics, he sang:

Lord,

I have done everything
you assigned to me to do,
sincerely.

Time for me

to return to you.

(Gānavardhini, *dayajūcuṭakidi velara)*

As his end approached, Tyagaraja wished to formally renounce the world and become a *sannyasin.*
Paramahamsa Brahmanandendra performed the rites and christened him Nādabrahmānanda. He duly gave his thanks to his Lord and acknowledged for one last time the dominion of the words and musical notes in his life:[19]

O Rama, thanks to your grace...
I am now in eternal bliss,
which is of the nature
of primordial notes
that adorn your form
and words which drape you.

(Yadukula Kāmbhoji, *nī dayace rāma)*

If anyone still wondered whether this supreme devotee was also a *jñāni,* he described the qualities of the Lord in no uncertain terms in his very last song:

Know for sure
the effulgence of the Lord

who is all the gods,
the elements, the creation;
the qualified, the unqualified,
the formed and the formless.

(Vāgadhīśvari, *paramātmudu velige)*

He then entered yogic trance and merged in his personal target.

---

[19] The chronology of the song may not be accurate.

Index of Songs in *A Companion*

(Initial long and short vowels are not distinguished in the alphabetization. Neither are s and ś.)

Alphabetical List of Songs in *Tyagaraja: Lyric to Liberation* and *A Companion*

(The initial Roman numeral is the volume number. I refers to *Tyagaraja: Lyric to Liberation*, and II refers to *A Companion*. The second number, the Arabic numeral, is the page number in the volume specified.)